D1479054

VILHELM MOBERG

THE UNKNOWN SWEDES

A Book About Swedes and America, Past and Present

Translated and Edited by Roger McKnight
With a Foreword by H. Arnold Barton

Southern Illinois University Press
Carbondale and Edwardsville

E
184
S23
M613
1988

Copyright © 1988 by the Board of Trustees,.
Southern Illinois University
All rights reserved
Printed in the United States of America
Designed by Studio Orest
Production supervised by Natalia Nadraga
91 90 89 88   4 3 2 1

Library of Congress Cataloging-in-Publication Data

Moberg, Vilhelm. 1898–1973.
[Okända släkten. English]
The unknown Swedes : a book about Swedes and America, past and
present / by Vilhelm Moberg ; translated and edited by Roger
McKnight ; with a foreword by H. Arnold Barton.
p.   cm.
Translation of: Den okända släkten.
Bibliography: p.
ISBN 0-8093-1486-X
1. Swedish Americans.   2. United States—Emigration and
immigration.   3. Sweden—Emigration and immigration.   4. Immigrants—
United States.   5. United States—Relations—Sweden.   6. Sweden—
Relations—United States.   I. McKnight, Roger, 1937–
II. Title.
E184.S23M613 1988
973'.04397—dc19   88-1731
                                                                              CIP

The paper used in this publication meets the minimum requirements of
American National Standard for Information Sciences
—Permanence of Paper for Printed Library Materials, ANSI Z39.48-1984. ∞

Contents

Foreword

There are no more avid readers than the Scandinavians, and none hold the creative writer in greater veneration. In Sweden, few authors have achieved such immense popularity as Vilhelm Moberg (1898–1973), whose four great novels about the early Swedish emigration to America, published between 1949 and 1959, are believed to be the most widely read works of fiction ever written in Swedish. They have since appeared in some thirty other languages. Masterfully translated into English by Gustaf Lannestock, they have enjoyed great success in America, reinforced by Jan Troell's epic film versions, *The Emigrants* and *The New Land*, from the early 1970s.

That Moberg's emigrant novels have struck such a chord of response derives not only from their literary qualities but also from the sheer magnitude of Swedish emigration to the New World. Except for Ireland and Norway, no European country experienced heavier emigration in proportion to its population, and there are few Swedes without kinfolk across the Atlantic. Moberg's novels brought into focus, as nothing else had done, the widespread, diffuse, yet deeply rooted views and sentiments of the author's people concerning the great exodus of recent generations. The Moberg version of this vast historic phenomenon is now firmly established in the popular vision of the national past in Sweden. It is as though his protagonists, Karl Oskar and Kristina, are part of every Swedish family.

Foreword

Building upon the success of *The Emigrants,* the first and ultimately the most popular of the series, Moberg brought out *The Unknown Swedes* in 1950, based upon articles he had previously published in leading Swedish and Swedish-American newspapers. This book further solidified his version of the emigrant experience. A new edition containing an additional, final chapter (included in this volume), came out in 1968. For those in the English-speaking world who followed Moberg's emigrant novels with interest and enthusiasm, it is regrettable that this commentary and supplement has not previously been available in translation.

The Unknown Swedes evolved during the first two years Moberg spent in the United States doing background research and writing *The Emigrants.* He took his research seriously; in time he came to consider himself as much a historian as a novelist, and he was so regarded by much of his devoted following. For this there was much substance, above all in his rare ability to combine creatively documentary study with imaginative insight and direct personal experience, most notably in dealing with life among the humble folk of the countryside. But he also showed the weaknesses of a powerful ambition combined with a relative lack of formal education. He made his share of mistakes, albeit largely in matters of detail; the editor's notes to this new English-language version of *The Unknown Swedes* point out errors he made in this instance. He tended, moreover, to view history in strongly moralistic terms and he did not hesitate to praise, or perhaps more often, to condemn.

Eager to appear the true discoverer of a vital, yet neglected and indeed deliberately shunned side of Swedish history, Moberg, while at times drawing upon their findings, was less than generous in recognizing the already extensive work of numerous Swedish Americans who for generations had devoted themselves to the study of the emigration and of the history of their compatriots in America. Among these were such scholars, by avocation or vocation, as Eric Norelius, Ernst Skarstedt, John S. Lindberg, Florence E. Janson, and Nels Hokanson, to mention

Foreword

but a few. He remained silent regarding the contributions of certain predecessors in Sweden itself, like Gunnar Westin or Albin Widén.

As Moberg claimed his place as a historian, he found himself judged accordingly, and he did not take kindly to criticism. He responded heatedly to those who pointed to historical errors in his treatment of the emigration and the Swedes in America. Similar controversy surrounded the appearance of the two volumes of his last, uncompleted work, significantly entitled *Min svenska historia*—literally "My Swedish History" although published in English under the title *A History of the Swedish People*. The "people," characteristically for Moberg, meant essentially the common people, as opposed to the high and mighty, among whom he included the professional historical Establishment, which denied him the final recognition he so avidly desired.

Moberg's triumph lay in his enormous success in appealing directly to the historical imagination of the broader reading public, both at home and abroad. If *The Unknown Swedes* is thus less significant as a work of historical scholarship than as a notable example of historical opinion making, it should nonetheless be recalled how much of what we presently know about the Swedish emigration and the Swedes in America is the result of an impressive wave of historical research that has taken place *since* 1950, in large part inspired—directly or indirectly—by Moberg's writings.

The Unknown Swedes is significant from another point of view. It is an important contribution to the rich genre of European visitors' descriptions and discussions of American life and culture. There are many notable Swedish works of this nature, from those of Israel Acrelius and Peter Kalm in the eighteenth century, to those of Axel Klinckowström, C. U. von Hauswolff, C. D. Arfwedson, and Fredrika Bremer in the earlier nineteenth century; Mauritz Rubenson, Ernst Beckman, Isadore Kjellberg, P. P. Waldenström, and August Palm during the era of the great migration; and Anna Lenah Elgström, Gunnar Myrdal, and Jan Olof Olsson after its conclusion.

Foreword

Like all such accounts, *The Unknown Swedes* is as much a commentary upon the author's homeland as it is upon the country visited, and like almost all of his Swedish predecessors Moberg was a social critic who contrasted conditions he found in America with those he deplored at home, even though he, like they, found much that seemed alien and unattractive in the New World. While admiring, above all, America's freedom, social equality, and the kindliness and generosity of its people, he was repelled by its materialism, corruption, violence, and cultural impoverishment.

Seen against the background of earlier European and Swedish commentary on America, one is impressed by Moberg's overall agreement with and further reinforcement of views long expressed by those who had journeyed to America before him. The extent to which Moberg had tended to idealize the American republic, even before arriving there, is revealed by the depth of his disillusionment during the Vietnam War, when he came to feel that those who held most faithfully to basic American ideals were those seeking asylum abroad, including in Sweden.

Finally, *The Unknown Swedes* is an important work for what the confrontation with a time and place other than his own tells us about one of Sweden's most protean cultural figures, who strove to reconcile within himself—in a manner perhaps more reminiscent of the nineteenth than of the twentieth century—the competing roles of artist, historian, and moralist.

H. Arnold Barton

Preface

This volume is a translation of Vilhelm Moberg's *Den okända släkten*. The book is an account of Swedish emigration to the United States and an evaluation of selected aspects of American culture. It was first published in Sweden by P. A. Norstedt in 1950 and reissued in revised form by Pan/Norstedt in 1968. A literal translation of the Swedish title is "the unknown relations" or, more broadly, "our unknown kinsmen," a reference Moberg intended for his Swedish readers with relatives in the United States.

This translation has been edited for English-speaking readers who have little or no knowledge of Swedish or conditions in Sweden during the nineteenth and early twentieth centuries. Wherever possible, I have retained the Swedish terms for Old World cultural phenomena and the titles of publications; I have included the English translation of these terms in brackets. In dealing with Swedish publications that have also appeared in English translation, I have included the English title in italics. In those instances in which the publication has not been issued in English translation, I have translated the title but without italics.

My reason for preparing this text stems from an interest in Moberg's depiction of rural life and his criticism of social conditions in both Sweden and America. I have been assisted in preparing the text by Paul Cole, who cooperated in the prelim-

Preface

inary translation of the final four chapters. I offer my thanks to Mr. Cole for this help, which he cheerfully gave despite the pressures of work and study. His contribution has been valuable not only for the work he did on the preliminary version but also for his continued interest in the text.

Grateful acknowledgment is extended to the Estate of Vilhelm Moberg for permission to publish this translation. A special note of gratitude is also due Gustavus Adolphus College. I have received a generous grant from the college's Centennial Celebration Fund, which has aided me in completing the project and in arranging for publication of the text.

Roger McKnight

Introduction

No modern Swedish author has been more widely read or controversial than Vilhelm Moberg. A man of strong opinion who described himself as "easily moved, hot-tempered, and changeable,"[1] Moberg lived in a world of contrasts. This is a fact that even a brief discussion of his career indicates. He was of humble rural origins and maintained lifelong contact with the farmers of his native province of Småland. Yet he spent most of his life near Stockholm, often involved in public debate over government corruption and inefficiency. From his youth, furthermore, Moberg supported collectivism and socialism. Still, as his thinking evolved through the years, he strove more and more to assert his independence and was most at ease with people from those nations that he viewed as the most individualistic. Moberg the novelist was intrigued by old-fashioned Swedish folk culture. He dreamed nevertheless of emigrating to America in order to make a name for himself and gain financial success in the New World.

Moberg grew up in a country that was in transition. Half a century before his birth (on August 28, 1898), Sweden was an agrarian society with a rigid class structure. While the landless poor comprised the majority of the population, the upper classes controlled the government and most of the nation's wealth. Mobility was limited by laws requiring passports for domestic travel and deposits of money prior to journeys abroad. In addition,

Introduction

religious freedom was restricted by ordinances that forbade devotional services outside the auspices of the State Church.

By the end of the nineteenth century, Sweden was well on its way to becoming a modern industrial nation with extensive urban settlement, a vigorous labor movement, and virtual freedom of religion. Far out in the countryside, however, were places where the old rural ways survived. One such area was Kronoberg County in southern Sweden, where Moberg spent his childhood. The general region was known as "darkest Småland" because of the people's conservative Lutheranism and reluctance to accept other religious views. Only one railroad station existed in the vicinity of Moberg's home, and the horse was still the most common means of transport. Clothes were produced locally and often paid for by barter.

Moberg spent his earliest years there in a small family cabin. His father, a career soldier, earned a meager government salary and farmed a plot of forest land. He and Moberg's mother came from families so poor that all their brothers and sisters emigrated to America. In the book *Berättelser ur min levnad* [Tales of my life] Moberg writes fondly of his childhood home, calling it the place "where I ran barefoot," and remembers the people who made lasting impressions on him. At the same time he recalls the frustration of trying to satisfy his hunger for learning in an isolated community where the school year was short, the teaching poor, and books scarce. Moberg's biographer Magnus von Platen describes the area as one "which must have felt like a prison for a young, highly gifted person. But at the same time it was the kind of place that can become the object of great longing for someone who has escaped from it, only to face the problems of a more troubled existence elsewhere."[2]

After trying his hand as a day laborer while a teenager, Moberg left his parents' home in 1916 to attend school at Grimslöv and later Katrineholm, both in southern Sweden. The Spanish flu, which nearly took his life, brought his formal education to an end in 1918. (Von Platen calculates that Moberg spent a total of only five years in school.)[3] Through his twenties Moberg worked

Introduction

as a small-town journalist, but in 1929 he moved to Stockholm and continued to make his home near that city until his death in 1973.

Moberg and the Emigrants

From the beginning of the 1920s, Moberg had devoted himself to his authorship. It was, however, the popularity of his 1927 novel *Raskens: en soldatfamiljs historia* [Raskens: the story of a soldier's family] that earned him his lasting reputation as an author for and of the common people. Set in Småland, the novel is a realistic portrayal of the lives of a professional soldier and his family. In 1929 and 1930 Moberg published *Långt från landsvägen* [Far from the highway] and *De knutna händerna* [The clenched hands], also novels with rural settings. These two books contrast their main character's, Adolf from Ulvaskog's, nineteenth-century values and resistance to change to his children's desire for modernity and social mobility.

This contrast between the old and the new remained a common theme in Moberg's writings. Once he had settled in Stockholm, however, he also became involved in debates about the social problems of his time. By principle a champion of the common folk and by temperament ill at ease in subordinate roles, Moberg attacked the Social Democrats for their perpetuation of the bureaucracy and their support of the State Church. Later, when World War II broke out, he criticized the Swedish government's failure to take a firm stand against nazism; his bestselling novel from 1941, *Rid i natt* [*Ride This Night*], though set in the seventeenth century, can be read as a comment on the tyranny of the Nazi era.

Raskens, Rid i natt, and other writings established Moberg's place among the Swedish working-class novelists [*proletärförfattare*] of the 1920s, 1930s, and 1940s. These authors, including Jan Fridegård, Ivar Lo-Johansson, and Moa Martinson, were the first in Swedish literature to describe the lives of the lower classes from the perspective of men and women who had grown up

Introduction

among them. Moberg's depictions of the customs and way of life among Småland's rural poor were his lasting contributions to this school.

Moberg continued his criticism of the Swedish government after the war. He saw corruption and favoritism behind the apparent stability of the nation. In the early 1950s he took a personal interest in several cases (the so-called Kejne, Haijby, and Unman-Lindkvist affairs) involving blackmail and cover-ups in the police force and legal system. His book *Det gamla riket* [The ancient kingdom], published in 1953, is a satire of governmental injustice that was partly inspired by the disillusionment he experienced in dealing with these cases. Later in the decade Moberg argued against the continued existence of the Swedish monarchy. The Swedish royal family was to Moberg a reminder of past autocratic rule, and he insisted on the establishment of a fully republican form of government.

As a result of these opinions, Moberg was viewed as a troublesome gadfly by many government and church officials. His general popularity as an author soared, however, due to the publication between 1949 and 1959 of the Emigrant Novels [*Utvandrarromanen*],[4] Moberg's tetralogy about Swedish emigration to the United States. Because of his aunts' and uncles' emigration, Moberg had been interested in the Swedes in America since his boyhood. He writes in *Berättelser ur min levnad* thåt reminders of America were ever-present in his childhood home. His family's relatives in the United States sent letters, photographs, American money orders, and Swedish-American newspapers home to the soldier's cottage in Småland, where they served as tangible proof of a world outside southern Sweden. With promises of financial aid from one of his uncles and with dreams of becoming an American writer, Moberg himself planned to emigrate as a teenager, only to be dissuaded at the last moment.

Still, the subject of emigration was fixed in his mind as the autobiographical novel *Soldat med brutet gevär* [Soldier with a broken rifle] gives evidence.[5] In the first part of this book, Moberg combines the experiences of his parents and those of his own youth and transfers them to the life of his persona, Valter Sträng. Valter, as a boy in Småland, sees his father die of diabetes (a disease that in reality had stricken Moberg's paternal grandfather). Valter's mother is then forced to give up the soldier's cottage where Valter and his brothers and sisters had been born, thus exacerbating the family's impoverished situation. One by one, Valter's siblings emigrate to America. Valter also considers emigration, but decides against it; he is the only one of the children to remain in Sweden. The fictional Valter, like the real-life Moberg, remains at home to keep Swedish traditions alive and to preserve the memories of those who left for the New World.

Throughout the 1930s Moberg made plans to write a fictional account of Swedish immigrant life in America, principally, if one accepts comments he made in 1966,[6] as a memorial to his relatives abroad. He wrote later: "I know that I have a genuine streak of stubbornness, a quality to be taken for better or worse. And I had made up my mind that I was going to cross the Atlantic Ocean in order to search out my unknown relations. For I could not get their destiny out of my mind. The older I became, the more it interested me."[7] It was not until after World War II that he began the project. Financed by royalties from *Rid i natt*, Moberg came to America in 1948 and did extensive research in New York, Philadelphia, and the Swedish settlements in the Midwest. Through museums, newspaper archives, and the personal reminiscences of Swedish Americans, Moberg found the materials that form the historical basis of the Emigrant Novels.[8]

These books have been read as a fictionalized documentation of the Swedish emigrant experience, and Moberg emphasized their historical verisimilitude by publishing a bibliography of his sources for the novels.[9] He portrays his characters as being forced out of Sweden by poverty, injustice, and religious persecution.

This epic story of Karl Oskar and Kristina Nilsson can also be seen as a psychohistory of Moberg's own generation. For Karl Oskar, who as a young man defies both parental and governmental authority in Sweden, emigration offers a hope for the

Introduction

future that he believes in with almost total optimism. For Kristina, who dutifully follows her husband to America, emigration entails the abandonment of age-old traditions and the loss of an ancient Swedish birthright. Through Karl Oskar's eyes, Moberg sees America as a land of economic opportunity for those with practical skills. Still he does not allow the reader to forget the lingering homesickness that Kristina feels for her native Småland. The ocean that separates Kristina and her family from home is remindful of the division between the old and the new that existed in the lives of Moberg and his Swedish contemporaries.

When Moberg came to America more than thirty years after his youthful attempt at emigration, he carried much the same cultural baggage as the earlier emigrants. His research visit to the Midwest was informative (four months divided equally between Michigan and Minnesota), but the climate and the way of life there presented him with formidable barriers. "I have difficulty believing that there can be more boring places on this earth," he wrote about the small towns of the Upper Midwest.[10] In the coastal cities of California, however, he found an unexpected haven. Moberg lived off and on in Carmel, Monterey, and Laguna Beach from 1949 to 1955 while writing the first volumes of the emigrant tetralogy.

During his early years in the United States, Moberg's attitudes toward Sweden and America were remarkably similar to those he gives his hero Karl Oskar. Memories of World War II lingered on in his mind. The numerous public debates he had taken part in at home were not yet dead issues. And *Det gamla riket* had not been popular with Swedish readers. With these frustrations, Moberg came to view modern Sweden as the same oppressive nation it had been a hundred years earlier. He wrote: "After all the disruptive battles which I had struggled through in Sweden . . . there grew up in me a deep-seated bitterness towards the Kingdom of Idyllia [Sweden]. During my life in exile [and] in light of the great distance [separating Sweden and America] I saw my homeland as a country of nothing but powerful enemies."[11]

Moberg rested his hopes instead on America. Here he found none of the Swedes' "obsequious respect" for high society and bureaucracy. "Democratic social behavior has been more fully realized in America than in any other country that I have visited," he wrote later.[12] There is evidence that Moberg had expectations of financial success in America. Gustaf Lannestock, his translator and friend from California, explains in his book on Moberg in America that the novelist eagerly awaited the American edition of *The Emigrants* in the hope that it would result in literary recognition for him in the United States and lead to economic independence. Lannestock writes that Moberg often claimed honor and fame were not enough for him: "He needed money, so much money that he could settle permanently in America." At another point Lannestock writes that Moberg "had dreamed of making a great breakthrough in America, both as an artist and as a 'moneymaker'; he wanted to become the most successful of all his family who had emigrated."[13]

Writing The Unknown Swedes

While he waited for recognition and as his funds from Sweden ran low, Moberg supported himself by writing articles on American and Swedish-American culture. He commented briefly on this arrangement nearly twenty years later: "In order to remain in the country [the United States] I found it necessary to write articles about America for newspapers back home. My friends Karl Ragnar Gierow of *Svenska Dagbladet* and Ivar Öhman of *Folket i Bild* rewarded me generously in dollars for my contributions to their publications."[14] These articles, collected and revised, form the backbone of *The Unknown Swedes*, first published in 1950 and reissued in 1968 with an added chapter, "Twenty Years Later."

Taken as a whole, the eight chapters in the 1950 edition of the book contain much of the (not unguarded) optimism that Moberg felt about the United States between 1948 and 1950. Comments on American principles of freedom, the nation's ethnic mixtures,

Introduction

the spirit of individual enterprise, and the confidence shown by the common people of the New World are all included in these pages. Moberg praises the legacy of the Swedish immigrants, including some of his own family members who settled in the Midwest and helped build the country. In "A Swedish Cemetery in America," he speaks of their toil and tribulation in military terms: "We have great victories to recall in America. But it should also be remembered that this great Swedish contribution has taken its toll of human lives" (p. 63).

By praising the humble newcomers in this way, Moberg invokes his own interpretation of history: he rejected the traditional heroes of the history books. To him the farmers who tilled the soil, the soldiers who fought the wars, and the women who carried on daily life were the true makers of Swedish history. Moberg brought this point into focus in 1968 when writing about characterization in the Emigrant Novels: "My characters were not supposed to be heroes of the Superman type, who acted as if they were conscious of their contributions as pioneers. I had decided to try to deheroify my portrayal of the emigrants."[15] This idea runs through the early chapters of *The Unknown Swedes*. To Moberg the immigrants were not heroes "bearing sword and shield and coats of mail; they were merely common folk in gray homespun" (p. 64). In his mind's eye he sees the first immigrants arriving in the Midwest with their wooden shoes, quaint manners, and near illiteracy, traits that were only offset by their practical skills and capacity for hard work. The best example of this type of hero is in "The Life History of a Swedish Farmer." Andrew Peterson, a jack-of-all-trades, typifies the humble but resourceful Swedish common folk.

At other points, however, the stoicism and staidness of the midwestern Swedes reminded Moberg of the less romantic aspects of the Swedish character. In "How the Swedes Become Americans" he looks back with distaste on the puritanical lifestyle and conservative politics of the old-line Scandinavian Americans. In "The Pioneers' Church" he voices his disappointment that the diligence of the midwestern Swedish Americans has not led to any other than material gain. He finds their cultural and religious life impoverished and bigotted.

Moberg had to travel to the West Coast before he found what he considered a felicitous combination of Old and New World culture. In the most-often-quoted passage from *The Unknown Swedes* (p. 108), he describes his first glimpse of California. The countryside seemed to him a paradise on earth. Lannestock describes Moberg's reaction to the contrast between the Midwest and California: "He thought that it was like coming to the Garden of Eden. Here were flowers and greenery—a few days earlier they [Moberg and his family] had left the Midwest, where the snow had already begun to fall, for it was November, the beginning of winter, which was the season of the year that he always had to suffer through."[16] In an interview with a Swedish correspondent in 1949, Moberg explained that the mildness of the climate in California and the freedom he had from the Swedish bureaucracy made him consider staying on the West Coast. He commented: "It seems as if the authorities here have greater respect for the individual than at home, and I like that. I wouldn't have anything against settling here for the rest of my life."[17] Moberg's delight with California extended to the Swedish Americans he met there.

"The Juniper Bush and the Orange Tree" records the culmination of the author's American journey. In what he calls the "last pioneer state," Moberg found the largest contingent of his "unknown relatives," and he was delighted by the ethnic mix they represented. Moberg touched on this point in the 1949 interview, in which he contrasted the way of life in California with that of the Midwest: "It was natural that the pioneer church was the gathering place when the immigrants first began to come over more than a hundred years ago, but how can it be that there hasn't been more of a change than has taken place? In the Midwest—I'm not talking about California now—it's as if nothing exists in between the church and the taverns in the Swedish settlements." He added that young people in California enjoyed greater freedom than those in the Midwest.[18] There is a note of awakened pride and vibrancy when he characterizes the children of marriages between Swedish Americans in California and other ethnic groups there (especially the individualistic Irish and Scots): Swedish tenacity has been complemented by "a versatile intellect and a lively temperament" (p. 122). California is the land of individualists where a new way of life is being created with the help of a revitalized Swede, an almost literal "new man" made out of diverse ethnic stock.[19]

The 1950 edition of *The Unknown Swedes* ends with the chapter "How the Swedes Become Americans." Although Moberg regrets the Swedish Americans' lack of knowledge about the modern world outside the United States, he praises American culture for its ethnic diversity, religious freedom, and democracy. In the Swedish cemetery in Minnesota, Moberg let his thoughts drift back to the Old World, which still bore the scars of two world wars. He writes: "Old Mother Europe starves—and young America hastens to the rescue" (p. 64). Moberg reaffirms this in his closing comments: the American people "stand out as the most powerful defenders of human freedom in the world today" (p. 128).

The Loss of Faith in America

The author Sven Delblanc has described Moberg's attitude toward America during the period when he wrote the Emigrant Novels: "During the 1950s Moberg entered into a period of rather näive romanticism about the United States. The realist, the writer Moberg, knew better and the epic framework [of the Emigrant Novels] leads on as usual to defeat and disillusionment."[20] Years before Delblanc wrote these words, Moberg came to a similar insight about his relationship to America. After 1950, complications gradually arose as the newness of his immigrant experience wore off. The first sign of difficulty was Moberg's realization that his attempt to become an American was destined to fail.

Introduction

We know from Lannestock and his American wife that Moberg's English was not good. Despite his years in America, he remained reliant on Swedish culture and the Swedish language for his inspiration. In contrast, Moberg's relatives in the United States were totally American, despite their Swedish ancestry. Moberg and his relatives were clearly products of separate environments. Moberg describes the situation in this way:

> No matter how comfortable and physically healthful my outward, purely material, existence seemed in California, American culture and life-style remained basically foreign and, in a way, repulsive to me. I belonged to Europe. As an eighteen-year-old youth, as an emigrant in 1916 instead of 1948, I could have been assimilated by the country and settled into the American way of life. In 1916 I was still a malleable person, but when I came to the United States, I was already set in my ways. I was too old to melt into this new environment. I was as unassimilable as an old piece of granite that had never changed through the millenia. I was an emigrant in America for seven years without changing the least bit; I had my emigrant visa; I could have stayed in the United States until the end of my life. But in 1955 I returned to Europe once and for all. . . . Thank God that I did so![21]

Moberg left Sweden but was unable to shed his Swedishness, an experience he often includes in the lives of his fictional characters as well. The ultimate impossibility of transferring one's deepest roots to new soil becomes, in fact, an important theme in Moberg's later novels. During his old age in Minnesota, Karl Oskar drifts in his thoughts back to the Sweden he had rejected four decades earlier. In addition, immigrant Albert Carlson, the main figure of Moberg's 1965 novel *Din stund på jorden* [*A Time on Earth*], spends his retirement alone in a California hotel room, after living nearly his entire adult life in America. With the sounds of the Pacific in the background, he dreams of his boyhood in Småland and laments his youthful decision to leave Sweden. Like Moberg, these figures are unable in the end to become totally American.

While Moberg does not specify what aspects of American culture were repulsive to him, the Americans' lack of respect for literature and the arts and their narrow view of world affairs were clearly sore points for him. In *The Unknown Swedes* Moberg mentions the disappointment of his more conservative American acquaintances when they learned that he was a novelist (see chapter 5, "The Pioneers' Church"). Moberg was also disturbed by the Swedish Americans' reaction to the first edition of his novel *Utvandrarna* [*The Emigrants*] in 1951. There were protests against the vulgar language used by characters in the book. Lannestock recalls that Moberg lamented at the time: "Is there no one in America who knows what literature is?"[22] The following years deepened his suspicions. When *Unto a Good Land* came out in 1954, Moberg found that sections from the original text had been omitted without his permission, at which time he is said to have exclaimed: "They have castrated my book!"[23] During the same year Moberg wrote to Lannestock that *Unto a Good Land* had appeared in the United States in a "strongly censored" version.[24]

The situation worsened when Moberg argued with Simon and Schuster about the proper methods of advertising his novels as well as the publishing house's choice of dates for publication. The final frustration of a personal nature came in 1955 when Moberg was temporarily forbidden to leave the United States until he deposited a sum of money with the Internal Revenue Service as a guarantee against possible back taxes. This measure surely reminded Moberg of the nineteenth-century Swedish laws requiring deposits of money by those wishing to leave the country. Lannestock reports that twice during this affair Moberg stated he would never return to America. In addition, Moberg wrote the following lines to Lannestock on different occasions in 1955:

Introduction

"So now the United States has begun to exceed Sweden in fantastic stupidity and bureaucracy"; and "it looks as if I have become a victim of the bureaucracy, both the American and the Swedish."[25]

At the same time, Moberg's personal problems were aggravated by his growing dissatisfaction with developments in American politics. In 1952 he was dismayed to learn that Charlie Chaplin had been forced out of the country for his leftist sympathies. Later he spoke out to journalists against the McCarthy hearings, but his comments never appeared in the American press.

After his return to Sweden in 1955 and up to the early 1960s, Moberg's comments about the United States were subdued. From his base in Sweden, Moberg spoke out, however, against the Soviet Union as it put down uprisings in Poland and Hungary. His first public protests against the United States did not come until the escalation of the Vietnam War. Beginning in 1965, he published articles in Swedish newspapers arguing for self-determination for the Vietnamese (see p. 133).

By 1968 Moberg's indignation caused him to append the chapter "Twenty Years Later" to the new edition of *The Unknown Swedes*. Here Moberg attempts to come to grips with the American trust in material progress and individualism that he himself had once been attracted to. Lacking a firm base in the humanities and practicing what Moberg calls a "vulgar patriotism" (p. 124), the Americans have uncritically accepted the image of a violent society as their national trademark.

Moberg pursues his idea that the political tables have turned between America and Western Europe: the political liberalism with which he confronts the Swedish Americans in 1966 clashes with the cold-war mentality of the American middle classes. In the end the only heroes Moberg discerns are those private individuals with the courage to protest against injustice. On the streets of Chicago during the 1968 Democratic National Convention, he sees a demonstration by young people who demand a return to the original principles of the American Revolution. But the note of optimism he expresses in re-creating this scene is dissipated by the darker tone of the final postscript.

Moberg's optimism had soured. He seems never to have forgotten his personal disappointments in America. This—coupled with the war in Vietnam, the American inability to counteract Soviet intervention in Czechoslovakia in 1968, and the election of Richard Nixon as president—inspired him with little hope for a renewal of the American spirit.

The 1968 edition of *The Unknown Swedes* concludes on a doubly pessimistic note. It is the work of a man writing his last words about a country that had occupied his thoughts since childhood; after 1968 Moberg remained silent about America. In addition, *The Unknown Swedes* leaves off where many of Moberg's other works begin—with an image of the common people caught between forces of oppression. Moberg writes: "The Soviet Union . . . has upheld its position as the greatest defender of oppression in the world. During the last three years it has sometimes appeared as if that position would be threatened by the United States. Now the balance has been restored" (p. 150). Moberg saw the dark sides of both Old World and New World leadership and could speak out only on behalf of the young and the defenseless.

The Critics

When the 1950 edition of *The Unknown Swedes* was issued, Moberg wrote to Lannestock expressing his pleasure at its popularity in Sweden. The 1968 edition was also well received. Still, the book has not been without its critics, especially among those who read it as a factual report on conditions in Swedish America.

In 1960, for instance, the linguist Einar Haugen called attention to Moberg's choice of mixed Swedish-English vocabulary in the Emigrant Novels. In his field studies in the Midwest, Haugen recorded the patterns by which Scandinavian immigrants incorporated English vocabulary and syntax into their native lan-

Introduction

guages. Moberg's fictional immigrants, however, speak a mixed language that Haugen described as "a free construction based on inadequate observation and understanding of the environment he [Moberg] has sought to describe."[26] This charge gave rise to the so-called language battle carried on for several months in the pages of *Svenska Dagbladet* in Stockholm.

Moberg defended himself against Haugen by claiming that he had based his immigrants' speech on the mixed language found in the journals of Andrew Peterson and cited several of the entries from Peterson that are included in chapter 2 of *The Unknown Swedes*, entries that Moberg claims in the text are unaltered from the original journal. Haugen later illustrated that Moberg's claim to exactness is inaccurate: nearly all of the Peterson entries supplied by Moberg in "The Life History of a Swedish Farmer" are either spelled and punctuated differently from the original or contain information not entered under that date by Peterson himself. Though Moberg continued to argue his case, the debate was never resolved, nor did Moberg satisfactorily explain the inaccurate entries he supplied from Peterson's journal.[27]

Another writer, the Swede Helmer Lång, has discussed historical inaccuracies in Moberg's text. In "A Swedish Cemetery in America" Moberg writes of discovering the grave of his grandmother's sister—Lena Stina—who Moberg says died in 1861. Lång shows that the woman buried in Minnesota, whose name Moberg later changes to Inga-Lena, is Lena Stina Svensdotter, who was born in 1817 and died in 1856. She was not a relative of Moberg, although she was from Algutsboda, Moberg's home parish. Moberg's actual great-aunt, Lena Stina Johansdotter, was still alive as late as 1905 and never left Sweden.[28] Lång describes Moberg's story of his long-lost relative as "a writer's beautiful invention."

Contradictions such as these in Moberg's text do not seem inconsistent with the author's personality. Moberg's self-characterization—"easily moved, hot-tempered, and changeable"—is complemented by other statements in which he describes himself as subject to sudden shifting spells of optimism and pessimism. In addition, von Platen has given a convincing portrait of Moberg as a dreamer and *fantasimänniska*, that is, an individual with the capability of forgetting the realities of the moment and immersing himself in the imaginative aspects of an event. The ideas of history were often most useful to him in that they excited his imagination and aided in the creative process.

Haugen and Lång were correct, of course, when they pointed out junctures in *The Unknown Swedes* at which Moberg disappoints his readers' demand for factual information. Still it is evident that two of the most imaginative moments in the book occur in the sections that Haugen and Lång take exception to. When Moberg reconstructs the life of Andrew Peterson (recapturing the spirit, if not the letter, of his writings), or when he stands in the cemetery in Chisago County and thinks of the impoverished immigrants who laid the foundation for modern America, the *fantasimänniska* is at work. At such moments it is of secondary importance whether he identifies individuals by their literally proper names or relationships. Although Haugen and Lång both admit that Moberg, in Lång's words, "has . . . on many points, with every right, allowed the demands of literature to triumph over the historical,"[29] they demand at other places a strict adherence to literalness when the subjective truths of the moment are the most important.

Most readers will find it essential to view *The Unknown Swedes* as a combination of social history and literary memoir. Like so much else concerning Moberg, this book exists on conflicting planes. There is a mixture of factual information and creativity, a tension between the past and the present, and a barrier formed by the differing mentalities of the Old World and the New. Moberg was unable to make a synthesis of these contrasts, but *The Unknown Swedes* is his attempt to bring about a better understanding of the diverse worlds of his Swedes.

The Unknown Swedes

Dedicated to Edgar Swenson,
friend and companion in America

Author's Note

The subject of this book is that branch of our Swedish national family that has settled in the United States of North America; the author has not felt it to be an exaggeration to describe these Swedes and Swedish descendants as *our unknown relations*.

Those sections that deal with Swedish settlement areas in North America were written on the spot. "How the Legend of America Was Created in Sweden" and "How the Swedes Become Americans" were written later and have not been published earlier. The other articles have appeared, in whole or in part, in *Svenska Dagbladet, Nordstjernan,* and *The American Swedish Monthly;* some of these appear here in this book in revised and expanded form.

V. M.

CHAPTER 1

How the Legend of America Was Created in Sweden

Just over a million people have emigrated from Sweden to North America. In this way, our country has been deprived not only of the emigrants themselves, but also of their descendants: those who emigrated took the future generations with them on their journey. The number of Swedish descendants in the United States today can be estimated—if one also includes the third and fourth generations—at a figure that stands somewhere between two and three million; probably about halfway. If the emigration to America had never taken place—if we imagine that all of these people had found a way of making a living in the country where they were born—then our Sweden of today would have *ten* million inhabitants instead of *seven* million.[1]

Nathan Söderblom[2] once described this emigration to North America as the greatest event in the modern history of Sweden. During the last five hundred years our country has waged many devastating wars, but this emigration has cost the country more people than all of those wars put together. In this light, Söderblom's words hardly seem exaggerated. What has happened during the last one hundred years is in fact nothing less than the splitting of our Swedish race into two branches, one of which is now disappearing into another culture, in another part of the

7

world. It is difficult to imagine an event with more far-reaching consequences for a people.

But strangely enough this great Swedish migration has been given a very obscure place by those who have written the history of our country. The only one of our historians who pays any appreciable attention to it is Carl Grimberg in his *Svenska folkets underbara öden* [The wonderful destinies of the Swedish people]. In the exhaustive *Sveriges Historia* [Sweden's history], which appeared in ten volumes under the editorship of Emil Hildebrand, there are approximately one and one-half printed pages on Swedish emigration to North America. And in the textbook on Swedish history that I once had to read in grade school there was not a single word on the greatest event in the modern history of our country.[3]

But during the first years of the twentieth century, the government authorities initiated an investigation into the causes of emigration to America. The task was entrusted to Professor Gustav Sundbärg.[4] By then emigration had already been under way for over fifty years, and it appears to us that this investigation was started somewhat late. But this made it all the more thorough. It was so thorough that it penetrated all the way down through the earth, to the loam and subsoil of every Swedish parish. When it was finally finished in 1913, it formed a gigantic work of twenty volumes. But when the *Emigrationsutredning* [Emigration Report] was declared completed, emigration had also practically ended. The following year World War I broke out, during which no emigration took place; between the world wars only a small number of Swedes left for America, but *the great flow* of emigrants had run out. It had reached its peak as early as the 1880s, when in some years the crowds of emigrants exceeded fifty thousand people, a figure equal to the present-day population of the city of Linköping.[5] During this time an average of one thousand Swedes left their homes every week.

Why? Why did the Swedes emigrate to North America? A great deal has been written about this question; it is fully answered by the *Emigrationsutredning* and will not be taken up here. I would only like to point out that the causes of emigration changed radically during the time emigration was going on. In its beginning, many were driven out of the country by the lack of religious freedom, the so-called Conventicle Decree [*Konventikelplakatet*] that forbade religious gatherings outside the sanctions of the State Church. This reason for emigration disappeared in 1858, when the long-standing ordinance was finally rescinded. But a new cause of emigration arose with the military statute from the year 1901, by which compulsory military service was considerably increased: during the first decade of the twentieth century, many thousands of young Swedish men journeyed to America in order to avoid conscription.[6]

But one of the causes of emigration seems to have remained unchanged through the past one hundred years, namely dissatisfaction with the bureaucracy and the civil service in Sweden and with all laws that inhibit freedom. This dissatisfaction finds eloquent expression among the first emigrants as far back as the 1840s. They leveled many hard and bitter words at the authorities here at home. "They make life unbearable in this country and are like a worm chewing at the fabric of society," writes one of the emigrants. And during my stay in America, when I met fellow countrymen who had emigrated in the 1940s, in nine cases out of ten I received the same answer to my question about their reason for emigrating: dissatisfaction with the authorities, with all laws and statutes that restricted liberty, with the civil service here at home. In the Sweden of the Four Estates, a personal, patriarchal oppression existed; in the Sweden governed by the Social Democrats, oppression is exercised by an impersonal, mechanically functioning government machine—that is the difference.[7]

Writers and emigrants themselves have, in other words, thoroughly analyzed and clarified what the Swedes emigrated *from*. And we can understand especially well the first emigrants who a hundred years ago left Sweden, the country of the Four Estates, a poor and underdeveloped land where the majority of the population was totally excluded from participation in national government.

But then another question arises, which no one has attempted to answer in detail: how did the pioneers know what they were emigrating *to*? Why did they believe that their lot in the new country would be a better one? On what did they base their hope for a more satisfactory livelihood in the New World? They were going to undertake a long and perilous voyage to a new part of the world, where they were to settle for the rest of their lives. They had made the great, crucial decision of their lives, and when they made it they must have been fairly convinced that North America could offer them a more tolerable existence than their homeland—that the change that was facing them would be a change for the better.

What did the first Swedish emigrants know about America? How had they gained their knowledge about the new country? During the course of my work on the novel *Utvandrarna* [*The Emigrants*], I was obliged to find the answer to these questions, whereupon I went to both published works and the preserved oral tradition.

During the previous century there appeared here in our country something that I would like to call the Legend of America. How was this legend created?

Two years ago the centennial of our Swedish-American pioneers was celebrated. But the special anniversary year of 1948 was rather arbitrarily chosen.[8] In fact a good many Swedes had emigrated to the North American Republic, as the new country was then called, several years before 1848, and the centennial ought to have been celebrated at least two years earlier; in the year 1846 the first large group emigration from Sweden actually began. This was undertaken from Hälsingland by the Erik Jansonist sect. Nearly one thousand of the sect's members made the crossing to America even before the end of the year 1846. These religious zealots were viewed almost as criminals by the Swedish authorities of that time, and the threat of exile hung

10

over their heads. Perhaps that is why it was not really considered suitable to celebrate the centennial of these pioneers' emigration.

It was during the 1840s, in other words, that emigration to North America became a social movement, and during the following decades it grew into a mass movement. Before that time it was only a question of an individual phenomenon, isolated cases: Swedes emigrated one-by-one, and their motives seem in most instances to have been solely personal. Some were attracted to the new continent by pure wanderlust or the love of adventure. A typical representative of these emigrants before emigration was Jacob Fahlström, called the first Swede in Minnesota. His life contains the elements of many exciting adventure novels. He was born the son of a potter in Stockholm in 1795; went to sea as a twelve-year-old; was shipwrecked on the coast of England but was rescued; wound up at last in Canada as a fur trapper and mail-carrier; became lost during an expedition into northern Minnesota; was captured by an Indian tribe; married a beautiful Indian girl, who bore him nine beautiful children; became so much a member of the tribe that he forgot his mother tongue and spoke only the Chippewa Indians' language; settled later as a pioneer on the spot where the city of St. Paul now lies; eventually became a Methodist preacher; and ended his days in the year 1857 as a missionary among the Indians. A couple of years ago Fahlström received a memorial stone in St. Paul. To our fellow countrymen in Minnesota, he is a great legendary figure in our time.[9]

The North American continent was also visited by Swedes who came merely to study it and describe it for those who remained at home. Carl August Gosselman, a lieutenant in the Swedish navy, undertook official exploratory trips across large areas of the New World, partly on assignment from the Swedish government. In 1835 he published an extensive narrative of his travels, *Resa i Norra Amerika* [A journey through North America], in which were gathered numerous facts about the great future land of emigration. Another travel writer was the merchant Karl David Arfwedson, a rather good writer, who can still be read without great effort. But his description of America does not delve deeply; he traveled mostly as a tourist and was content with the impressions of a tourist. The most important study trip to the States at that time was, of course, that undertaken by Fredrika Bremer in 1849–51. The epistolary journal *Hemmen i Nya världen* [*The Homes of the New World*], which she published after returning home, is in a class of its own from a purely literary standpoint.[10] Fredrika Bremer delved more deeply into American life than any Swedish traveler up to that time; she had a positive attitude toward the young republic, but she both admired and criticized conditions there. Her authority was great, and her book certainly contributed in a great degree to the formation of her readers' ideas about the New World.

But these travel writers were not emigrants. They themselves had not lived the life of a pioneer. Neither did their books ever become popular reading material, in a true sense. Fredrika Bremer was read by most so-called cultured people in Sweden, but the emigrants to America did not come from those circles. Other than in exceptional cases not even her book about America seems to have reached the impoverished Swedish common people who were contemplating the idea of emigrating. Furthermore, one should remember that the ability to read was by no means universal in those segments of the population from which the first emigrants were recruited. In the year 1842, when elementary school became obligatory in Sweden, they had already passed school age. And the birthdates on their gravestones, which I have seen in America, tell us that to a surprisingly great extent the first emigrants had already reached *middle age* by the time they set out upon the ocean.

But as time went by, the emigrants themselves came out with various books on their new homeland. One remarkable emigrant was Gustaf Unonius, known as the first Swede in Wisconsin and as the author of the most valuable account of Swedish pioneer life in North America that we have in our language. He was a university graduate. He had studied law and medicine at Uppsala before he undertook his emigration, in 1841. In his

The Legend of America

Minnen [Reminiscences] he relates that he and his wife were the first Swedish citizens who took advantage of the right, "that had recently been granted citizens of Sweden, namely to leave the country without special royal permission."[11] He describes how he was attracted to the journey: "America—what was there to prevent me also from going to that country, which like a new El Dorado appears before every venturesome youth? Her fabulous birth and history had excited our wonder from our earliest school years, when we learned to point out its position on the map." But at the same time he admits that before his departure he knew, as he writes, "extremely little" about conditions in that country, and adds: "In general, our undertaking was considered something extremely strange. To be sure, I cannot deny that even to me, with our limited resources and our scant knowledge of the country to which we were going to establish a home, the venture, when I gave it more serious consideration, seemed exceedingly risky."

After a few years, Unonius abandoned the settlement, Pine Lake in Wisconsin, that he had founded, and obtained an education as a minister in the Episcopal Church. In his book, mentioned above, *Minnen från en sjuttonårig vistelse i Nordvestra Amerika* [*A Pioneer in Northwest America 1841–1858*],[12] he highly praises the almost unlimited freedom that exists in the new republic and the complete equality with which people deal with each other. He argues that frontier life breaks down all differences between social classes. But Unonius also lets us know how hard, toilsome, and demanding it is. He himself could not endure such a life in the long run. Unonius was clearly a wilderness romantic; before he entered the primeval forests of the Northwest, he had never worked with his hands. And he emphasizes at many points in his book that this country is, above all, a land for manual laborers, not for other people. Here a man must be able to handle a plow and a spade, an axe and a saw. He specifically warns non laborers about pioneer life in North America and advises them against emigration: they run the risk of perishing in the unmerciful wilderness.

13

Another emigrant from the educated classes was Colonel H. Mattsson. He also recounts his *Minnen* [*Reminiscences*] and relates that he knew very little in advance about the country that he emigrated to.[13] He writes: "What we knew was that America was a new country with a free and independent people, that it had a liberal form of government and great natural resources." Despite the fact that both Unonius and Mattsson belonged to the more educated circles in Sweden, their knowledge of America was extremely limited. And other classes of people—precisely those who provided the great mass of emigrants—knew, of course, even less about the country.

Everything indicates then that a hundred years ago the United States of North America was *by and large still an unknown country* to our people. That much bolder and more adventurous seem the deeds of the first emigrants. By their more cautious countrymen they were surely viewed as daredevils and their emigration as a hazardous adventure, something "extremely strange," as Unonius expresses it.

In the beginning, rumors about America spread across the Swedish countryside, tales of hearsay and the like spread by word of mouth. At that time the Swedish common people also began to read newspapers; the small-town press had gained importance.[14] A few households would go together on the cost of a newspaper, which would then be passed around among the farms and read by each family in turn. And in these newspapers there was often information from the New World. Especially in 1848 there appeared many announcements and articles that told how people had found large quantities of gold over there—in the Sacramento Valley of California. People learned that the governor of the state had to prepare his meals himself— all of his servants had fled to the gold fields. Hundreds of thousands of gold seekers rushed there from all the countries of the world. In the popular imagination there grew up the legend of "the land of gold" off in the West. In several newspapers in Småland, for example, there appeared a news item about two farmhands from the parish of Mo who had returned from California with several bags stuffed full of pure gold, gathered in a very short time. After these farm laborers had exchanged their gold for Swedish currency, each purchased a Swedish estate of his own for the exact amount of his money. We can understand the effect such news had in the impoverished rural areas.

In the 1840s the first so-called emigrant societies [*emigrant föreningar*] were founded in Sweden. Everyone who intended to emigrate to America was eligible for membership. These associations published small informational brochures on the United States for the benefit of prospective emigrants, who therein found advice about the crossing, about what they should take with them on the journey, how they should acquire land in the new country, and so forth. Of course, the New World is painted almost solely in enticing colors. It is said, however, that this continent is principally suitable for "industrious farmers and craftsmen," who are especially encouraged to emigrate.[15]

But a true book about America for the people had been missing up to this point. Such a book did not appear until 1853. It was published in Växjö by "the widow Denreu," and strangely enough the author himself had never been in the country that he described. The book is written by a minister from Småland, Vicar Johan Bolin of Sjösås parish in the diocese of Växjö. The popular tradition in the district remembers him as a rather mediocre cleric and preacher. But in one field he was a unique person in the country at that time: concerning his knowledge of America. I wonder if there was any Swede living at home a hundred years ago who knew more about the United States than Vicar Bolin. All of his knowledge was the fruit of reading, but the depth of his reading is impressive. He supplies a bibliography of approximately seventy works about America, published in several different languages.

Vicar Bolin writes in the introduction that his book was "the first of its kind and extent in Sweden." "For," he makes it clear, "this description is published not for the learned who know much, but for the Swedish people in general and the unlettered— particularly future emigrants." The author wishes to tell our

15

people what the United States is like, as guidance for those who intend to emigrate. He feels that those who have already emigrated have been uninformed—they have not had any other knowledge of the country than that which they have been able to "acquire through rumor, personal letters, newspapers or pamphlets." This work was meant, in other words, to fill a need that had long existed among our people.

Vicar Bolin's work would seem to be the first popular, complete description of the North American Republic to appear in Sweden. Its complete title is: *Description of North America's United States, in respect to its natural state, animals, plants, minerals, manufactures, economic means, government, judicial system, religious life, educational institutions, military power, commerce, means of communication, welfare system, taxes, burdens, with natural historical and other information; along with special details and advice for those who wish to immigrate there.* And in order that the contents shall not appear to the reader as fabulous and exaggerated, the author lists all of the sources from which everything is gathered.[16]

Bolin's factual information and description of actual conditions in America appear for the most part to be accurate; the book is painstakingly written. But the author accepts nearly everything in the New World at face value; the whole amounts to an oversimplified and strongly idealized portrait of the country: all institutions in this republic—political, economic, ecclesiastical, social—are better than their counterparts in Europe. The system of government is the best in the world, "for the good of the people and the proper development of human capabilities," he explains. The United States maintains no costly military establishment and pays salaries to no "useless office clerks and civil servants." And although he himself serves as a minister in the Swedish State Church, he praises the free churches in America, where the pastors do not comprise a privileged class. Vicar Bolin adheres to the principles of total religious and civil freedom that had been realized in the New World; in this respect he was more tolerant and unbiased than his contemporary colleagues within the Swedish State Church. And his liberal opinions were not to keep him in the good graces of the cathedral chapter in Växjö.

But in another area, the author shared the prejudices of his time: he does not react to any appreciable degree against slavery. He explains that the Negro slaves are treated very well and that they have a more tolerable lot in life than most of England's factory workers and most farmers in Europe. And in this republic, he writes, there is no type of aristocracy, no kinds of princes or princesses, no court or courtiers—except for the slaves there are only *citizens*, all of whom have the same rights and who are distinguished from one another only by their different professions.

Those readers who intended to emigrate took most notice, perhaps, of the book's reports on the prosperity that they could attain over there: settlers harvested crops of blessed abundance, which after a few years made them well-to-do or rich; a carpenter's helper received a salary of seven hundred *riksdaler*[17] a year over and above meals in the home of his master; a common farmhand earned more than one hundred dollars a year; and a servant girl in the United States could get just as high a yearly salary as a farmhand, "without, in general, doing any other work than that which is, for all that, extremely light." For women emigrants there was, in addition, a very special benefit that could be attained: "But better than all salaries in cash is this truth, that foreign serving girls, and other women, who are beautiful, healthy, and capable, without independent wealth, get married quickly and advantageously in America." This was, of course, an advantage that could not be measured in money, and the information on marriage prospects was essentially correct: at that time a great shortage of women existed in America. Nowadays there is a normal supply of women even there, but in some places the concept of the United States as the country where "every girl gets married" still lives on. I believe that we have here a contributing factor to female emigration, which has been overlooked by the *Emigrationsutredning*.

The communications systems in America are, according to Bolin, the most expedient in the world, and especially the railways are described as a great marvel. Aside from a few experiments with horse-drawn cars pulled along tracks laid down in the ironworks of Värmland, railways were still unknown and untried in Sweden. In North America they already amounted to a length of nearly ten thousand miles, and over there steam was then being used as a propellant, with the consequence that the trains could travel at the miraculous speed of over twelve miles an hour. The steam coaches run on eight wheels to keep them from derailing, and each one is equipped with fifty to sixty comfortable seats as well as a stove that gives off a pleasing warmth. In addition, each coach offers a convenience that makes it unnecessary for the passengers to get out of their coaches. Several coaches are linked together in a row, but at the end of each coach is a small bridge over which, during transit, one may pass from one coach to another if one wants to meet an acquaintance. In some coaches, there are special small family berths and a stewardess to serve the travelers. In other cars, there are treats and refreshments, which are carried around by a steward during the journey. Railway journeys are described as a great form of popular entertainment.

Among the wonders of the United States, Bolin also mentions the world's largest picture, an oil painting that is three miles long. An American, Mr. Wanward, working completely alone with oil colors, has painted the entire Mississippi River on canvas with cities, villages, shorelines, elevations, forests, and islands. The painting, Bolin writes, is "surprisingly like the object." The artist had exhibited his work in London. How he arranged for an auditorium for the purpose of exhibiting this canvas, three miles in length, we are never told.

Vicar Bolin's book was widely distributed and read among the classes of people for whom it was intended, and the image it gave of America could not help but make an impression: the work of this pastor from Småland certainly added to the multitude of emigrants. *Description of North America's United States* is

one of the most important works in the history of S\
igration—it must have aided powerfully in creating the Lege\.
of America in Sweden. Vicar Bolin himself never went to the
States, but he surely contributed to the increase in the country's
population.

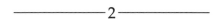

——————— 2 ———————

Our first emigrants consisted for the most part of landowning
farmers. Due to the large increase in population among the peasantry, the size of their farms decreased steadily, and the number
of landless persons doubled and tripled in a short time.

But the very poorest people in the rural areas still had no
significant place in the stream of people that left the country.
The reason was, quite simply, that these people lacked the means
to make the crossing. Crofters, migrant workers, the landless
poor,[18] and similar people had to stay at home for the most part;
their time came later when communications had improved and
the entire process of emigration had been simplified and become
less expensive. A few farmers paid the passage for the hired folk
they intended to retain, but it is told that farmhands and serving
girls left their masters and mistresses only too quickly in the
new country and made a go of it on their own.

The landed farmers were, in other words, the pioneers of
Swedish America. Settlers from Hälsingland, Dalarna, and Småland were in the forefront of the trek. Closely following were
farmers from Östergötland, Västergötland, and Halland.[19] Here
it was a matter of family emigration: they traveled with their
wives and children. At times they joined up with relatives, neighbors, and acquaintances from the same parish to form a larger
group. A hundred or more people might band together to cross
the ocean. Later on, such groups had as their leader a Swede
who had returned from America in the capacity of an emigrant
recruiter.

The largest and most notable group emigration in our emigrant
history was undertaken by the so-called Erik Jansonists. Because

19

of the consequences it had later, this phenomenon is highly important to our subject.

Erik Janson was a farmer's son, born in 1808 in Biskopskulla parish in Uppsala County. He too became a farmer and made a name for himself as an enterprising agriculturist. While he was out working in his fields one day in the year 1834, Janson was called by God: he fell down on his face like St. Paul; he himself relates that he was hurled forward into a ditch. Thereafter, his life was extremely eventful during the next sixteen years until it was ended in the year 1850 by an assassin's bullet in a court-room in Cambridge, Illinois, in North America.

Erik Janson felt himself to be the chosen prophet of God; during the latter part of his life, he looked upon himself as a new Christ. His preaching cannot be explained here.[20] On crucial points, however, it stood in opposition to the pure Evangelical Lutheran faith, and out of this arose his conflicts with the authorities, the worldly as well as the spiritual. Janson went to Hälsingland as a traveling wheat flour salesman, and in those rural settlements he soon attracted so many followers that his conduct aroused great concern among the clergy. He taught that the Bible was the only book that counted for a Christian. All other writings were false and misleading and should be burned. A hundred years before nazism, Erik Janson organized book burnings in the parishes of Hälsingland. But it was not decadent and immoral literature that he burned; it was Luther's, Arndt's, and Nohrborg's sermons which he had thrown to the flames.[21] For his book burnings he was indicted and put under arrest. During the course of his work in Sweden, Janson was arrested six times, and once he was set free by his followers during a transfer of prisoners. For long periods he lay hidden in the homes of his followers, wanted by the authorities. There occurred regular battles between his sympathizers and the local inhabitants.

This situation proved unbearable in the long run; Erik Janson's sect was prevented by the Conventicle Decree from practicing their religion in their home parish, and in time the plan arose for a mass emigration to North America.

The Legend of America

An individual emigrant had written some letters to his home parish in Hälsingland, and these letters were to show important results: they gave Erik Janson the idea to emigrate.

A man from Alfta parish by the name of Gustaf Flack had journeyed across the Atlantic in the year 1843, and he had traveled as far westward as Chicago. Flack is considered to be the first Swede to walk the streets of the town that was destined to become the foremost Swedish city in America.[22] In his letters home to Alfta, he gave a glowing description of the new country. He expatiated especially on the total religious freedom that existed. There was no state church, no inquisitory and tyrannical ministers to torment the people—America was a home for all, where each and every one could worship God according to his own conscience. The letters circulated among friends and acquaintances in his home parish. And it is reported in a contemporary work: "These letters filled the tormented friends of Erik Janson with new hope."

But Erik Janson himself was obviously not totally convinced: he sent one of his principal followers, the freeholder Olof Olsson, to America with the assignment of inspecting the country more closely and sending home reports.[23] This, along with many other of the religious founder's actions, indicates that he was by no means an introverted and impractical dreamer who went around immersed in an otherworldly reality. Just the opposite: everything indicates that Janson was a practical and capable man who had a firm grasp of worldly affairs, and he gave particular proof of a great organizational ability. The enterprise that he planned was also far from being of the easiest kind.

Olof Olsson set out on his exploratory journey in the year 1845. He traveled to those parts of North America which at that time were considered the Far West: he traveled through Illinois, Wisconsin, and Minnesota. This emissary sent home to his leader good reports on the country and enthusiastically encouraged emigration. He was especially impressed by Illinois and considered that state as the most suitable place for settlement.

21

Erik Janson hesitated no longer: he now decided to travel to America himself, while his followers were to come later. Before his departure, he described America to them as the Promised Land, where they would be able to eat figs, wheat bread, and bacon: "For wild swine are there in such profusion that one only need shoot, slaughter, and eat." In that land all the people lived in harmony as a single large family. Of course there were also fierce beasts in the wilderness, but snakes and dragons could not harm the chosen people of God.

Janson had now decided that he was going to build the New Jerusalem in North America. He was going, as it was said, to "turn unto the heathens of the New World inasmuch as the inhabitants of the fatherland did not want to accept and believe the truth."

In July of 1846 he arrived in America, where he was united with his emissary and sympathizer, Olof Olsson, who as a scout in the foreign country had done good work. Together now they were to pick out a suitable spot in Illinois for the New Jerusalem. They decided in favor of an area in the vicinity of Galesburg, approximately one hundred miles from Chicago. The settlement was named Bishop Hill after Janson's home parish.

The so-called Erik Jansonists, the farmers from Hälsingland and Dalarna, emigrated in eight different groups in as many different vessels during a period of seven years, 1846 to 1853. Their emigration came to be a great tragedy, the greatest tragedy in our emigrant history, as far as the passage itself is concerned. Altogether approximately one thousand five hundred people followed their master and prophet across the great ocean. One of their vessels went down and everyone aboard was lost; it quite simply disappeared en route and was never heard from again. About two hundred persons died during the crossing from various diseases, especially cholera and scurvy. In addition is the fact that many died after arriving at their place of destination. The high death rate was due to a large extent to Erik Janson's having forbidden his people to consult doctors: he who believed and asked God for help, he would be cured; he who did not believe was not worthy of anything but death.

This pioneering adventure reaped a grim harvest of human lives. Many pitched battles with fewer casualties have been dealt with in detail by our historians, but one searches in vain for information in our history books about the fate of these farmers from Hälsingland and Dalarna.

Erik Janson founded a communistic society at Bishop Hill, where all property was to be held in common. This community was dissolved after a few years, and then the colony was run with great success on the basis of other and freer principles. As previously mentioned, the founder himself was assassinated as early as the year 1850 by one of the many enemies that he had made.

The contemporary assessments of Erik Janson and his deeds are, naturally, extremely varied. To his host of followers, he was the "great light" whom God had sent into the world to enlighten its people, Christ revealed in a new bodily form here on earth. Some of his disciples believed that he, like Christ, would rise again from the dead. But his antagonists called him an unconscionable scoundrel and an enticer of the people, a notorious deceiver and seducer of women. What was the truth? Without accepting his followers' messianic portrait, a present-day observer who attempts to be objective must admit that his detractors' description of him is nowhere near to being exhaustive. Even if most of his qualities seem unsympathetic, he somehow arouses the reader's admiration. Anyone who, through his teachings, could induce one thousand five hundred people to risk their lives on the dangerous ocean voyages of that time cannot, at any rate, have been a run-of-the mill person. Janson seems to have been a man who towered far above those around him, a preacher with a hypnotic power over his audience, who has few counterparts within our popular religious movements. In America he is considerably better known than here at home. On his grave stands an imposing memorial stone; there is a detailed biography of him in English; and Bishop Hill, the settlement that he founded, has been written about by several American cultural historians.[24] The new country has seen him in a more favorable light than his homeland has. His settlement did not become the New Jerusalem, of course: Erik Jansonism never became a force in the spiritual life of America. But the Erik Jansonists made a major contribution on a purely material plane: these farmers were capable and knowledgeable and hardworking agriculturists, and as tillers of America's soil, they carried out an achievement that is lasting.

I have recently gone through around sixty letters that Erik Janson's followers wrote home to Sweden and that have been preserved in the Uppsala provincial archives.[25] To the extent that these letters accurately describe life in the new colony, it appears obvious that Erik Janson governed his little kingdom with absolute dictatorial authority. He was martyred for the cause of religious freedom in his homeland, where his actions contributed to the repeal of the Conventicle Decree and were, naturally, of historical importance, but how far his own tolerance of people holding differing views extended is apparent in the book burnings that he ignited. It must certainly be said that the farmer from Biskopskulla was one of those not-unknown champions of liberty who love liberty so dearly that they see no other alternative than to try to keep it for themselves.

Now what do the Erik Jansonists' letters tell us about America? This is the question that most closely belongs to our subject. And this much can be ascertained immediately: if there is anything that has given circulation to the Legend of America in Sweden, then it must be these letters from Bishop Hill in Illinois.

One is first struck by the fact that these sectarians are more literate than the Swedish common folk in general one hundred years ago. Most of the authors of the letters I have read express themselves fluently in writing. The style of the letters is biblical; the images and metaphors are borrowed from the Bible. Throughout long sections, a person has the feeling that he is reading the Holy Scriptures. Here is an excerpt from a letter,

The Legend of America

dated the 12th of July, 1847; it is from a son writing to his parents
who live at home:

"I wish now in my fortunate and happy situation to let You
know something about this country's inestimable bountifulness,
about its great riches, about the general welfare that exists in
every house and cabin. It is truly a Canaan where milk and
honey flow to each and every person who is able and willing to
work. The climate is temperate and healthful, the air unusually
high, fresh, and clear, long warm summers, no cold autumn
and spring, the winter short, only about three months, the land
rich and fertile, covered with deep loam, fertile to such a degree
that I need not fertilize it, but need only every year harvest her
rich crops that I have planted. Here there are no crop failures,
but everything yields a rich dividend. The Americans are a good
people, friendly in their dealings and treat strangers and foreigners as friends and brothers.

"A few words to You, my beloved parents: You shall not think
of me with pain, sorrow, or concern, but rather be happy and
embrace me in Your loving memory, for I find myself in good
and fortunate circumstances, I live in a generous and rich country, among honorable and good people and have good earnings."

It is fully understandable that the lush and fruitful land would
appear overwhelming to farmers from the meager and rocky
Swedish countryside. The comparison with the land of Canaan
recurs in many letters. This letter writer's description of the
climate arouses some surprise, however; he fails to mention a
word, for example, about the intense and unremitting summer
heat right here in the Midwest which I personally have had very
unpleasant experiences with. It takes a couple of years before a
Scandinavian manages to acclimate himself in these parts, and
it actually happened that a number of the first emigrants died
of diseases that were caused by the climate.

One of Erik Janson's principal representatives, the freeholder
Anders Andersson, has written to Hälsingland letters both nu-
merous and lengthy, addressed to a farm foreman named
Ekblom, who to some extent seems to have sympathized with

the sectarians. At any rate, he had clearly been of assistance to them. From Andersson's letters I cite some excerpts typical of the colonists' mentality and of their view of America:

"I can now tell You that the Word is made manifest unto us and all of our enemies' prophecies are come to naught. For the country that we have occupied is such a country that we have no earthly wants. The Lord has shown us the way and prepared a place for us, and we live now in secure dwellings and in great contentment. We are blessed here in the new world in both a bodily and spiritual sense.—This country's laws are different from the laws of our fatherland. Here we have the protection of the worldly law as well as of the worldly authorities. Each and everyone of us has the right to serve God according to his own conscience. Here we are allowed to listen undisturbed as Erik Janson explains the Bible. For the light which God has lit through Erik Janson cannot be hidden either in prison or the madhouse. But Sweden is and shall remain a House of Darkness.

". . . Nor do we ever need to have physical want here. If we plant a barrel of corn, then we reap five hundred barrels in return. So is God's word made manifest unto us: We who have forsaken everything for the sake of the Scriptures are now rewarded a hundred times over.

". . . Let those People whose names are written below hear this letter of mine according to its contents! I wish to send warm greetings to my father to say that I and all those close to me are so well that you could not believe it."

There is a note of triumph throughout these colonists' writings: they have found a new and better mother country, and they gloat over their adversaries back home who have predicted misfortune for them. In some cases, the names of a number of people in the home parish who are to acquaint themselves with the contents of the letter are specified; in other cases, they are to be made known to as many people as possible in the area. Their eagerness to disseminate knowledge in Sweden about the sect's present good fortune in America is genuinely touching. "We who were despised in our native land have risen to great esteem

26

here," a colonist writes at one point. "The people of this country are greatly astonished at us."

Another of the colonists, Per Andersson, writes from Bishop Hill in the year 1851, five years after his arrival in the country:

"I can now mention to You that we have reached a high degree of prosperity, and here in this huge country there is room for all of You, if you wish to make the crossing. The land here will not give out for many hundreds of years. You ought to have a little extra money, however, when you arrive.

". . . The journey over here costs rather a lot, but those who can and have the means to make the move, they will not regret it. I advise everyone who is able-bodied to get started on his way over here, away from the slavery of Sweden, where not even with the cleverest calculations can a person make his living."

Letters of this type passed from hand to hand in the home provinces of these travelers to America, and they could have had only one effect: continued emigration. It is obvious that the emigrants' letters, more than anything else, contributed to the creation of the Legend of America in Sweden.

Every new emigrant also became a new letter writer. In this way, the number of America letters increased more and more, as emigration increased. These letters were like pebbles thrown into the water: because of them waves arose that flowed out in ever-widening circles.

One emigrant, a former common soldier from Småland, Johan Dahlberg, writes a detailed letter to his former company commander, dated the 2nd of January, 1854, in which he dwells especially on the low prices of foodstuffs in North America. He gives a long list of examples: a person can get a barrel of wheat flour for twelve *riksdaler* Swedish currency and a "fat Goose" for twenty shillings.[26] "And good Distilled *Brännvin* is sold here for thirty-two shillings a Jug," Dahlberg writes, whereupon he adds in the next sentence: "I humbly beseech you to give my greetings to my Commander. Lieutenant, please convey this declaration for me—that I am better off here than serving as a Swedish Soldier. No one have I met who regrets his journey here, and it is said that many of my fellow countrymen will be coming here next year. I hope they do not regret their journey either."

I have read several hundred of the letters that emigrant Swedes wrote home to the old country, but from most of them there has been hardly any information to be found about the lives of the emigrants. The America letters are, as a rule, wholly conventional: the writers say that they are in good health and feeling well and the recipients are wished the same good gifts from God. Concerning their daily life and habits, the letter writers are reticent for the most part; seldom does one catch a glimpse in the form of a concrete picture. Misfortunes, suffering, and tribulations are not hushed up, of course, but they are generally touched upon with a light hand, most often for the natural reason that the writer does not want to cause worry and anxiety for those at home. On the other hand, the favorable occurrences are overexaggerated. Occasionally one has a feeling that the emigrant embellishes the details of his existence to the best of his ability. Only in exceptional cases does it happen that someone admits that he or she has failed in the new homeland. Ill fortune and sickness bear the blame for the adversities. Often there is more to be read between the lines than in them.

A few things might be said about the psychology behind the America letters. As objective, purely informative documents about conditions in America, they are of limited value: they are colored by each individual letter writer's temperament, level of education, religious viewpoint, occupation and environment—and especially by his origins and surroundings in Sweden. Almost without exception they assure us, however, as the soldier Dahlberg did: I have never regretted that I came here. America is seldom subjected to any criticism; the new country takes precedence over the old, if any comparison is to be made. There are few exceptions to this rule. This situation is also easy to explain psychologically, regardless of whether or not it is based on fact: the decision to emigrate is once-and-for-all, sacrosanct; it is not to be regretted. Even if the emigrant, in his heart of hearts, is disappointed and admits that his aspirations have come to nothing, he does not want to admit that the great, crucial decision of his life proved to be an unfortunate decision.

The emigrant does not regret his decision—and in the overwhelmingly greatest number of cases there probably did not exist any reason for him to do so either.

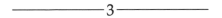

—————— 3 ——————

During the final years of the 1860s, the *great* emigration from Sweden to North America began. At this point, crop failure and years of famine here at home became powerful motivating forces. And it was during these years that Småland became the province of emigration ahead of other parts of Sweden. In the rural areas of Småland, the year 1868 still lives on in the memory of the people as "the hard year." During the whole of that summer hardly a drop of rain fell, and in many places the grain never reached the point of forming ears. Once again bark bread was placed in the oven. My mother, who was born in 1864, traced her very earliest memories back to 1868, when she thus was four years old. She used to tell how she went out into the fields with her mother and picked handfuls of hazelbush buds, which were baked into the bread.[27]

Many of the poorest inhabitants of Småland died from malnutrition during those years. It is reported, for example, in a chronicle from Långasjö in Kronoberg County, dated the 9th of December, 1868: "This past week the church bells rang here for ten corpses. Of these two had starved to death and one frozen to death." In a news item from Skede parish in Jönköping County from the same period it is announced: "Several farmers' children are going around and begging. More than four hundred people from this parish have emigrated to America during the most recent years. This has also enervated the people here, and crime lurks in the shadow of adversity." In the newspaper *Snällposten* from Malmö, for the 5th of May, 1869, we find the following telling news item: "During these days the city streets have swarmed with emigrants, who are making their way to America.

Last Wednesday six hundred farmhands and serving girls from Småland arrived here by special train. The emigrants were, almost without exception, young and hearty people."

In certain areas of Småland, emigration to America became nothing less than a mass folk migration. From Kronoberg County alone during the years 1850–1910, no fewer than sixty-two thousand people emigrated to America, or on the average somewhat more than a thousand people a year. (By way of comparison, it might be mentioned that the population of the whole county today is approximately one hundred and fifty thousand people.) It happened that half the number of inhabitants in a parish emigrated. Freeholdings and tenant farms were left deserted, and deep in the forests the small cottages of the landless poor were emptied of their young people—only the old and decrepit remained. The way led

. . .
västerut, där solen strålar över fria människors land,
västerut, där inga trälar kväljas under snöda band,
västerut, där människovärdet varder erkänt dock till
slut,
västerut, där flit ger ära, flit ger makt—
gå västerut!
[. . .
Westwards, where the sun shines over the land of
the free,
Westwards, where no one is enslaved in vile chains,
Westwards, where human worth finally receives its
reward,
Westwards, where diligence gives honor, diligence
gives power—
Go westwards!]

There are innumerable emigrant songs from that time. Emigration had become the great folk movement that also took expression in lyric form. America was honored and glorified in great numbers of broadsides, which were distributed across the

country. In most cases the authors of the songs are unknown.
One of the best-known and most-often sung ballads is "Emigrantens avsked" ["The Emigrant's Farewell"], whose final verse
reads:

> Farväl, o moder Svea! Nu reser jag från dig
> och tackar dig av hjärtat att du har fostrat mig.
> Men bröd du gav så ringa, det ofta ej förslog.
> Fast många av den varan du gifvit mer än nog.
> Nu draga vi som fordom från dig till fjärran land,
> utöver havets vågor, långt bort till Västerland.
> Där är ej ont om brödet, när man vill bruka flit—
> Vi tacka må Kolumbus, som viste vägen dit.

> Farewell, oh Mother Sweden! Now I journey away
>   from you
> And thank you with all my heart that you have
>   fostered me.
> You gave me little bread, often it wasn't enough,
> Although to many people you gave more than they
>   needed.
> Now as in bygone days we travel to the western
>   land, from you,
> Over the waves we go, away to foreign shores,
> Where there is no problem about bread if one applies
>   himself;
> We must surely thank the explorer who showed us
>   the way here.[28]

Emigration was, in its beginning, a completely spontaneous
popular movement that bore the imprint of necessity. But during
the final decades of the nineteenth century, it lost some of this
characteristic: it became, to an extent, a commercialized and
organized phenomenon, from which many people earned their
livelihood. The great folk movement was then also stimulated
by artificial means: a very purposeful *agitation* for emigration to
the United States of North America began to be carried on. This
was connected with the development of communications sys-

tems. There arose several new steamship lines, which competed for the passengers. The era of the emigrant agents arrived, and the Swedish countryside was inundated with people who offered America tickets for sale and who took out their fixed commission for each person who emigrated. In Gothenburg in the year 1871 a newspaper, *Amerika*, began publication, whose platform was to promote emigration. And now the passage itself was no longer the same perilous and complicated enterprise that it had been a quarter of a century earlier. With the new steamships it could be made in just as many weeks as it had required months during the age of sailing vessels. And in addition came the fact that the journey was now both cheaper and more comfortable. As time went by, the very poorest people could scrape together the money for a ticket to America. And a large number of those who had already gotten a foothold in America paid the passage for their relatives at home. In this way many thousands of Swedes who otherwise would have been compelled to remain in their homeland came to join the great host of emigrants.

There were, in other words, many factors working concurrently that then made emigration easier. It is also against this background that we should consider the high figures during the 1880s, the decade that saw more Swedes emigrate than any other in our country's history. It is also evident that the tariffs on grain drove a good many people of the nonagricultural populace to America—this is what it says in an emigrant ballad from the 1880s, "Emigrantens farväl" [The emigrant's farewell]:

> Vi aldrig frossat uti fina bullar,
> men vant oss vid försakelse och nöd.
> Och dock man kommer med livsmedelstullar,
> för oss fördyrar man ett magert brod.

> [We never feasted on fine cakes,
> But accustomed ourselves to abstinence and need.
> And yet now they come with food tariffs.
> And make more dear our meager loaf.]

The Legend of America

By this point in time, the Legend of America had become fully developed in Sweden. America was no longer an unknown country to the Swedish people in general. The emigration pamphlets, with their tempting descriptions of "the land of gold," had spread to the cottages and been carefully read. The letters from America had accomplished their meaningful work. Relatives from America began coming back to visit in the old country, and they told tempting things about their new homeland. In books, letters, and by word of mouth there appeared embellishments of emigrant life and idealized descriptions of the United States, but when all the exaggerations had been scaled away there remained one basic truth, which was tenable enough: for capable and industrious people America still offered greater opportunities than their homeland.

And around the turn of the century, it seems that the authorities in Sweden finally began to open their eyes: they began to see what was happening, and they began to comprehend the import of the immense loss of people that Sweden had had to sustain for half a century. So at last the anxious question was raised: What shall we do to combat emigration to America?

One of those who wanted to awaken Swedes to reflection was K.-G. Ossiannilsson. In a well-known poem he spoke of the debilitating loss of blood that Sweden suffered through emigration—of the "thousand reddish drops" that dripped away day after day:

> . . . tusen, tusen, åter tusen . . . !
> Vem skall tända stuguljusen?
> Tomma stugor stå i natten—
> allt ditt liv förrinner, Sverige,
> livet rinner ur ditt öppna sår.
> [. . . thousands, thousands, upon thousands . . . !
> Who shall light the cottage lamps?
> Empty cottages stand in the night—
> All your life blood drains away, Sweden,
> Life drips from your open wound.][29]

——————— 4 ———————

In my childhood I heard the story of a crofter in our parish who had come to the minister in order to make a death announcement. The crofter had just received the news that one of his sons off in North America had passed away, and now he wanted to announce this and ask the pastor of the congregation to hold final rites for the son. The pastor answered that he could do nothing about the matter since the deceased had not been an official member of his congregation but had died in his new place of residence in a foreign country.

The crofter then replied in amazement:

"But he lived in America! Since when is America a foreign country?"

We have sought to trace these developments from their beginning and have seen how America worked its way deeper and deeper into Sweden. In the end it worked its way so deeply into our country that an episode like the one related above could occur: the land in the west had changed faces; it was no longer a strange and unknown country; it had turned into the country where our relatives lived—in half a century it had been transformed into *a nation of kinsmen*.

And it was in this incarnation that America appeared in the Småland soldier's cottage where I was born just before the beginning of the new century. I have a very vivid memory that America was present in my surroundings—that it existed within the tenant cottage. I heard tell of America everyday. On the dresser top, the most conspicuous place in our home, stood the portraits of all our relatives in America, holy objects that were not to be touched; on a picture that hung from the wall were the words "Minne från Amerika" [Remembrance from America]; almost all the letters that came were sent from America; all the money orders came from America; the newspapers that we read were published in America and were sent to us from there, and so on. It would not be saying too much if I said that America had moved part and parcel into my childhood home—in the same way that it had moved into many thousands of other small cottages in the rural areas across our country in those days.

America was no longer a land of fairy tales here in Sweden; it was no longer a legend—it had become everyday reality.

And since more people of Swedish origin reside in that country than in any other country outside our own, that country concerns us more than any other outside Sweden.

CHAPTER 2

The Life History of a Swedish Farmer

Swedish pioneer life in North America is still a rather unexplored area. We know remarkably little about the lives of our first emigrants after their arrival in the new country, and about the conditions under which they made their new homes and a new life. They themselves related little about this; those men and women from among the Swedish peasantry who came to America during the first phase of emigration were not people of the pen. They wrote no books. They knew how to plow fields, build houses, do carpentry work, lay bricks, spin and weave; they could make their own implements and household goods, they could prepare the leather for their shoes and the cloth for their clothes and, if they had not possessed these skills, then they would have perished in the endless wilderness. They truly lived a life that is worth depicting. But these pioneers—as a later age calls them—lacked the education necessary to recount their own life history.

There is one notable exception to this rule, however: a Swedish farmer's life history, a voluminous manuscript that is preserved in its original form in the Minnesota Historical Library in St. Paul. It consists of notes in journal form that give a complete picture of a settler's and farmer's life in Minnesota during the last half of the nineteenth century, from the year 1854 to the year 1898. This gigantic diary seems to me to be of absolutely indispensable value to our knowledge of early Swedish settlement in the Midwest.

The above-mentioned library in St. Paul has a "Manuscripts Museum" that contains a large collection of manuscripts dealing with Minnesota history. One day in the summer of 1948, when I inquired about chronicles that dealt with the history of the Swedes in that state, a librarian came forward with a few volumes that in terms of format and binding seemed strangely familiar to me: long and thin books with spines of black cloth and with brown-speckled covers. They reminded me at once of those books that village shopkeepers back in Sweden normally have lying close at hand on the counter for entering the day's sales on credit. This was said to be the journal of a Swedish farmer by the name of Peterson, the librarian explained; he himself had no idea of the contents since he lacked any knowledge of Swedish, and he did not know if any other person had read the journal either. But perhaps it could be of some interest to me . . .

There were three volumes that had been given to me, containing entries for the years 1854–1875. I had not read far in them before I was filled with a burning desire to learn more about the author. His name was Andrew Peterson; the people at the library knew scarcely any more than that about him. I succeeded, however, in tracking down the place where Peterson had once had his farm: Waconia in Carver County, Minnesota. When I realized that this place was only about thirty miles from St. Paul, I made a trip there. In Waconia I met a Swedish-born ex-farmer, now eighty-seven years old, who had known the journal's author when he was alive. He showed me the way to the local cemetery where Andrew Peterson is buried together with his wife and his nine children. The gravestone informed me that he had not died until the year 1898, and the old man who had been acquainted with him firmly maintained that he had written in his journal up until the last day of his life.

In other words, up to this point I had seen only a small portion of Andrew Peterson's work. I then began to search for the missing parts of the journal, and in time it turned out that the Minnesota Historical Library also owned them: seven more volumes turned up! After their father's death Peterson's children had donated the entire work to the library. From 1875 onward, Peterson had kept a special "Memorandum Book of Incomes and Expenditures," which amounted to three volumes. Each of the ten volumes, which together constitute the whole journal, contains approximately three hundred pages, very closely written pages in large folio format. The entire diary is, therefore, a work of three thousand large, handwritten pages. In published form set in 10-point type on normal-sized pages, Andrew Peterson's journal would swell out to a gigantic volume of around ten thousand pages.[1]

So at last I had gotten the complete work in my hands, and I hardly believed my eyes when the ten volumes lay before me on the table in a foot-high stack. A half-century of pioneer life in Minnesota is contained in this pile of books: for forty-four years, from 1854 to 1898, Peterson has made an entry every single day. We probably have no counterpart to this gigantic farmer's journal at home in Sweden.

There are, of course, Swedish farmers who have written journals during a large part of their life; for my part, however, I have not met any. This chore is not among the most ordinary with Swedish common folk. And if Andrew Peterson had remained in Sweden, he probably never would have hit upon the idea of putting his daily experiences into writing—of sitting down and writing every day for half a century, on about sixteen thousand occasions. But the move to America was the emigrants' great, incomparable adventure in life. What they encountered during their transplantation to the foreign soil of America was totally strange to them, as different as it was from life in their home parish. He who happened to know how to write wanted to record it. Andrew Peterson knew how to write. The most astonishing fact, however, is that he managed to carry on his journal-writing enterprise for all of forty-four years.

A Swedish Farmer

But about the remarkable farmer's former life in Sweden the people in Waconia, his place of settlement, knew nothing. Strangely enough, all of his nine children had died childless; that is to say, the American branch of his family has already died out. A younger farmer from the area had heard that Peterson was supposed to have come from Östergötland, but he himself was a third-generation Swede and he thought that Östergötland was a church parish or possibly a town in Sweden. Judging from the language in the journal, I tried to guess at the author's birthplace, and I found a few dialect words that indicated that he could have come from Östergötland or northern Småland.

After I had published my first article on Andrew Peterson's journal in *Svenska Dagbladet*, further detective work was superfluous, however: the cathedral organist from Skara, Ivar Widéen, solved the mystery surrounding the author's earlier life. In a letter to the newspaper, he was able to inform me that Andrew Peterson was his relative, his maternal grandfather's oldest brother. He had never before heard of Peterson's journal, however; it also turned out to my great surprise that its existence had been totally unknown in Sweden up to this point.[2]

With the help of Mr. Widéen and after further research in Minnesota, I procured some data on the old settler from Waconia:

Andreas Peterson[3] was a farmer's son and he was born on the 20th of October, 1818, on the farm Sjöarp, a one-quarter unit of crown tax land,[4] in the congregation of Västra Ryd in the county of Östergötland. He is thought to have emigrated in the year 1850, possibly in 1849. In other words, he was a man in his thirties at the time of his emigration. About the very first years of his life in North America nothing is known.[5] But on the first page of his journal, he comments that he had taken out his first *nattjonal Papper*—citizenship papers—in the spring of 1853. He was then a resident of Burlington, Iowa. And from the following year onward, we are able to follow his life day-by-day in his own handwritten entries all the way up to the day of his death.

In Burlington, Peterson had joined a small group of Swedish Baptists, who had recently emigrated. The leader of the group was a former sailor from Halland, Fredrik Olaus Nilsson, known as the first Baptist in Sweden. During one of his voyages, he had had himself baptized in Hamburg, and in the year 1847 he began recruiting proselytes to the Baptist faith in his homeland. The result of his preaching was that he was exiled from Sweden in 1851 for violating the ordinance concerning unlawful assemblies, the so-called Conventicle Decree of the 12th of February, 1726, according to which it was forbidden for "males and females, old and young, known and unknown, few or many, to congregate and come together in private homes under the pretext of holding devotional services." For violations of this law, fines were imposed, the first time of two hundred Swedish *daler* in silver currency, the second time of four hundred *daler* in silver currency, and if the offenses were repeated a third time the guilty party could "for two years be exiled from the kingdom." Owing to enforcement of the Conventicle Decree, Nilsson was forced, therefore, to emigrate to America—he returned to Sweden, however, in 1860—and in Burlington he founded a small Swedish Baptist congregation. In the summer of 1855, most of the members of this congregation moved into what was then Minnesota Territory; they settled next to Lake Waconia, which is located in Carver County. (Today the town bears the name Waconia after the lake.) One of these newcomers to Minnesota was Andrew Peterson.

The new Swedish colony seems originally to have consisted of only eleven people. In Peterson's journal we hear the members' typically Swedish first names: there are Maja-Stina, Jonas Petter, Petter Danjel, Johannes, and so forth. The leader and pastor of this tiny congregation, the ex-sailor F. O. Nilsson, is referred to as "mister Nilsson" and his wife is called "missis." Both husband and wife set up a residence, with much of the work being done by their followers. But even Pastor Nilsson has staked a *kläm* and works the land. They are all farmers, even if one or another of them has learned another profession in Sweden; one member of the colony, for example, is reported to be a tailor. And everyone in this group of Swedes has set himself the goal of making a new home for himself in Minnesota, which had enough land for them—and, in this part of the Territory, very fertile land.[6]

But the Swedes are not alone in the area. Most of the settlers in Waconia seem to be Germans. Andrew Peterson takes over his *kläm* from a German and pays for the land—160 acres—with twenty-five dollars in cash. The seller is referred to in the journal as *tysken fisser* [the German Fischer]; incidentally, he furnishes bulls to breed with the Swedes' cows.

Andrew Peterson is certainly no wayward and helpless person in this foreign country. He seems to possess all the capabilities that are demanded in a pioneer settlement where, on the whole, a person starts out empty-handed. Peterson builds houses and makes furniture; he lays bricks for fireplaces and slaughters animals; he is a shoemaker, wagonwright, roofer, fruit-grower, syrup-boiler, vintner, and who knows what else. Over and above these jobs, he of course carries out all the normal chores of a farmer. He notes how during the course of one and the same day he has done carpentry work on his cabin, worked on a table, grafted fruit trees, completed the work on a hayrack, and slaughtered a sick heifer. But he does not boast over these many-sided qualities of his. Nothing would be more foreign to him than to point out his accomplishments as unusual, and in truth they were not uncommon in those surroundings. Peterson is what we in Småland call an *allehandamakare*, a jack-of-all-trades. He possesses those all-around manual skills that typified Swedish farmers in times past but that in our century of specialization have almost completely disappeared among them.

In Peterson's three thousand pages of entries, we are able to follow life in the colony day-by-day, year-after-year, decade-after-decade. Everything that is of importance from his viewpoint is written down, first and foremost the different chores of the day. The settlers in Waconia have set up a rational system of shared labor and help themselves by helping each other. They exchange day labor; people turn to their neighbors for the work that they themselves cannot do, while they do the neighbors a comparable favor in kind. In the journal we receive thorough information on the change of seasons and the more remarkable happenings in the weather: "the Biggest Rain I have seen in my days fell today"; "today there was Such Heat that we did nothing"—and so on.

Peterson is a bachelor at the time of his immigration but soon enters into marriage with a colony member by the name of Elsa. The wedding is reported as laconically as possible, in just under one line. The newly married man continues in the next line with a note that on that day he had also begun "plowing for wheat." For a farmer a wedding day is a workday like all other workdays. In Andrew Peterson's journal there is no room for personal confessions and outpourings. He never comments on an occurrence, no matter how important it may seem to us; he merely records it. He is only a chronicler, an extraordinary chronicler with his expressive colloquial language. This unlearned man has powers of concentration of great proportions. He writes briefly and concisely and unaffectedly, and his writing style remains unchanged even when it is a question of life's most important events.

His wife Elsa bears him children—nine of them—and at each delivery he briefly notes the child's name and the stroke of the clock at its birth. This takes up one line—and in an equally large amount of space he reports that a cow in the barnyard has had a calf. Only once, upon the arrival of the first baby, does he go into the matter in somewhat greater detail and devote a whole line to telling that he "was inside all day" and that "Everything is in good order." Concerning Sundays, Peterson reports only the fact that it was Sunday on that date; if anything noteworthy has happened on a Sunday, then the occurrence is usually entered in the note for Monday: the sanctity of the Sabbath is consistently upheld.

The family grows but at the same time we also follow the increase in the number of farm animals, in the cattle barn and pigsty. Each time a cow has a calf, a sow has pigs, or a ewe bears a lamb, then there is a note about it, and we are told, of course, how many pigs the sow had and if the cow had twin calves. There are several entries about the heifer *Fröken*, who after giving birth to a calf "didn't become clean," and Peterson returns three times to a sick calf before he is forced to write down that he "buried the dead Animal" today. But death also occurs among the people in these surroundings, and then it is Peterson who makes the coffin. Births and deaths among people and animals, burials, weddings, religious services, purchases, sales, trips to town, the mating of the animals, slaughter, plowing, threshing, rain, thunderstorms, blizzards, snowfall—all these are the pattern of life in the colony in Minnesota's virgin land, and everything is brought together here in life's own composition. Therefore it also gives the reader an overwhelming impression of originality, of truth. We believe every word that Andrew Peterson writes down in his *Dag Bock*, purchased in the city of *Sant Pall för 95 cänt*.

He notes down every bit of income and every outlay he has, may the sum be ever so small, which gives the manuscript a special value as a history of the times: we learn what everything costs; the prices of implements, tools, clothes, wheat, potatoes, bacon are carefully recorded, and we can follow the changes in trade conditions as the years and decades go by. The amount of factual information in these three thousand large pages is overwhelming. But about life outside Waconia little information is given. The Civil War devastates North America for four years, but here in the southeastern corner of the new state of Minnesota the people live in the most profound peace. Peterson writes only on one occasion that he has been found to be too old to go to the war; that is toward the end of the tremendous conflict, in the beginning of the year 1865, and he was then forty-seven years old. And the only political item I have been able to find is an entry from the 3rd of November, 1868: "We then voted for grant for President."

The settlement increases its material prosperity; new buildings are built; the old primitive cabins are replaced by more solid dwellings. A church and a schoolhouse are built, and Peterson bolts rafters into place and works as a carpenter. Later when examinations are to be held in the school building, he sits in as a witness. He becomes a trusted man in the area and is assigned to sit on the jury at the county courthouse in Chaska, although with concealed distaste: he comments once that he succeeded in "Being freed from the jury." His activities within the Baptist congregation are reported on but do not take up a great deal of space in the journal: they are referred to only when people hold meetings and baptisms, and a few times there are entries about *Bröds brytelse* and about *Kärleksmåltid*, words referring to communions and devotional dinners. In one poignant passage it is recounted about the Swedish colony in Waconia that "we have held Prayers this evening for our newborn Children."

Once it is observed, as though it were something unusual, that "two Germans" had themselves baptized. The baptisms took place in Lake Waconia; the Baptists believe, of course, that the entire body has to be immersed in water in order for a baptism to take full effect. The names of the visiting preachers are entered, as well as the fact that Peterson, on some occasions, donated "A dollar for the Preacher."

Strangely enough, however, the journal's author does not give the slightest impression in the gigantic manuscript he left behind of being a free-church man, in any case not of the type we know of in Sweden. Instead a person conjures up the picture of an Old Testament patriarch and man of the earth, a faithful tiller of the soil, unshakable in his faith in God and never-failing in the practice of his religion, but at the same time uninhibited in his affirmation of life and open with all his heart to the joy of worldly things.

Peterson improves his fortunes on his farm slowly but surely. Year after year the amount of cultivated land is increased by plowing new ground, and he and his sons drive increasingly fatter and heavier hogs to the meat market in St. Paul. Minnesota's dark loam yields marvelous harvests. The results of these harvests, which he carefully records after the threshing every fall, clearly reflect his mounting affluence. And the farmer's precision is absolute: he does not write in complete carelessness that he got around six hundred and forty-five bushels of wheat, but that he got six hundred forty-five and one-quarter bushels.

When we get into the 1890s and old age is near at hand, the chronicler himself fades into the background. Now it is his grown sons who have taken over the heavier work on the farm, and it is their daily doings that are recorded: "The boys did the plowing, the boys were to town." About himself Peterson writes more and more often: "Did nothing today, was not well." Or else he says: "Did all sorts of Small chores." Hundreds of times, especially in the later years, this splendid summary of a farmer's workday, which in most cases includes so many different chores, recurs: "all sorts of Small chores."

Every year Peterson bores into his sugar maples and collects their flowing sap, from which he boils syrup—one year more than a hundred gallons. This job was clearly his last. On the 26th of March, 1898, while he was "boring in the maples," as was normal at that time of the year, he was taken so seriously ill that he had to be carried to his bed. He died five days later, on the 31st of March. In the last entry he put to paper, he remarks that his sons are hauling fertilizer, that he himself is in bed, and that the weather outside was clear but not mild.

Not a word about the illness that broke him, not a syllable about his possibly imminent death; not with one word does he betray his thoughts on his deathbed. Instead he writes about his fields, which he has claimed from the wilderness with his own hands in a strange land and which his sons are fertilizing for spring wheat, and about the day's weather, which is of importance for the spring planting.

Andrew Peterson undeniably maintains a style of his own up to the very end.

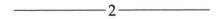

———————— 2 ————————

Andrew Peterson's journal is written in a language that presents major, and at times insurmountable, obstacles for even a

Swedish reader: a peculiar mixture of idiomatic Swedish, exclusive Östergötland dialect, and English. On the whole, the so-called *svensk-amerikanska*, the mixed language of Swedish emigrants, appears in these writings in fully developed form, it seems to me. Most likely the author of the journal has created a few of his expressions himself; in any case they had only just been adopted into the language as early as the 1850s, when Swedish settlement in North America was still completely new.

No language is easier to ridicule than *svensk-amerikanska*, and indeed it has often been put to use for that purpose. And in America this language stumped me many times with its curious turns of expression and its creation of new words. I recall how the bartender in a tavern in Minneapolis leaned over the bar and with an expression on his face that well bespoke his words confided in me: "You see—förra sommaren losade jag mig min kära hustru" [You see—last summer I lost my dear wife]; I recall how the wife in a Swedish-American family where I was invited as a dinner guest appeared in the doorway with a beaming smile on her face and said: "Vassego! Nu har jag puttat fram fooden på tablet!" [Please come to dinner! I have now put the food on the table!]. But if one considers the living conditions and opportunities of our emigrant countrymen more closely and works from their fund of knowledge at the time of their settlement in the new country, then one is not tempted to make a display of their language merely for "the fun of it." Then one feels rather that there is something unusually poignant about *svensk-amerikanska*. The emigrants—and especially the first ones—had gotten very rudimentary instruction in their mother tongue in their homeland. Generally speaking, they spelled this mother tongue very poorly. They were not masters of their own language when they came to the strange land. And there they were faced with a new language, completely different from their old one. But they had more to do than learn English: in the first place they had to support themselves. So on the basis of necessity these new means of expression arose—the emigrants themselves created a language with which they could get along in the new country.[7]

The emigrants' language can be characterized as a Swedish that met with the influence of English, mixed with an English that met with the influence of Swedish. A common feature of *svensk-amerikanska* is that those verbs that it has borrowed from English are conjugated according to the rules of Swedish: for example, *losade* [lost], *puttade* [put], *makade* [made]. Moreover, we find that the nouns retain the Swedish definite article, even though they come from the English: for example, *tablet* [the table], *lighten* [the light], *railroaden* [the railroad]. In Peterson's journal, we find many of the expressions that now definitely have been included in the special vocabulary of Swedish America. When he repairs the fence, then he writes that he *fixar fänset;* when he clears off stubble in the fields, then he writes that he *grubbar på filen* [grubs in the field]; when he prepares lumber, then he *makar lågg* [makes logs]; when he goes to a meeting, then he appears at a *miting;* and when there is a presidential election then he *votar* [votes]. To this point the reader encounters no difficulties with interpretation. And even when farmer Peterson writes that he *fixsade Räls* [fixed rails], one understands at once that he was not laying railroad track, but was chopping fence posts or slats (rails). But in his journal there are a number of word puzzles that I—despite consultation with experts on *svensk-amerikanska* in America—still have not succeeded in solving. No competent individual, for example, has been able to inform me what the journal author's wife Elsa was actually doing when she *fikade taike.* Personally, I guess that she was quilting a cover. Also, the nature of the farm implement that Peterson calls *kvädlen* still represents an unsolved mystery to me as well as to all the experts I have consulted.[8]

The farmer from Waconia writes the way he speaks; he spells his words phonetically, as they sound to his ear, which gives his entries an extremely genuine tone and a special actuality. He often employs a rich, dialect-colored language whose wealth of vivid expressions—sometimes forgotten in Sweden—has given me much pleasure. Here, for instance, I encounter a word such as *delasjon*—taken by the common people from the Latin of the appeals court judges—which I heard my grandmother use during my childhood. It means *exemption,* a grace period on a payment: "Mister Nilsson har fått delasjon med sitt kläm" [Mister Nilsson has been exempted from payments on his claim].

In the *Emigrationsutredning* were reprinted several hundred America letters that unfortunately enough have been paraphrased in standard Swedish and from which the *svensk-amerikanska* thus is weeded out. I consider this procedure to be a great mistake; due to the paraphrasing, the originality and colloquial tone of the letters have, to a large extent, been lost. I would not for anything on earth want to see Andrew Peterson's journal revised and reworded into just such a formal, watered-down Swedish.

In those excerpts from the journal that are published here not one letter is changed, not one punctuation mark moved, added, or deleted. But of course these short excerpts cannot give an accurate or fair idea of the contents of a work of three thousand closely written folio pages, which above all owe their effect to the assembled weight of the entries, to the mass of facts, to the immense wealth of objective information. Here I have selected some characteristic entries from eight different years in the Swedish farmer's life. Peterson repeats himself often. When haymaking is in progress six days in a row, then he also makes the same entry for six days: "Baled and pitched Hay." In order to avoid such repetitious comments, journal notations as a rule are not reproduced from consecutive days.

———————— 3 ————————

From Andrew Peterson's Journal:
1855

January:
27   fixed tables and made chairs to have in the church.

A Swedish Farmer

February:
5 I was in Town, bought Material for Trousers for 2:90, a Straight Razor for 95 cents, Writing paper and envelopes for 15 ct., Snuff for 10 Cent.

13 butchered Hogs, among other things,

14 in the morning cut Up Hogs, in the afternoon worked on the Shanty.

16 Salted pork.

March:
1 finished with the Cabinet and sawed out planks for the hay rack.

2 began at 7 o'clock in the morning sawing out boards for the hay rack and worked till 11 o'clock, when I became Sick with the fever.

3 bought wine and quinine for 5 cent.

4 Sick, bought quinine again for 50 cent;

13 Somewhat well, worked on the hay rack and Sent a letter to Sweden Paid 22 cents for half payment of the Letter.

27 was in town, bought 2 pairs of Stockings 80 ct., Fixed a Lock 25 ct., bought Drops 10 ct., Material for trousers 75 ct., Memorandum Book 35 ct., Ditto a Little one 5 ct., as well as Snuff 10 cent.

June:
19 I hoed and planted potatoes on my claim, got Alexander and Jonas Petter as well as Johannes to help me.

30 It rained, I cut rafters and small beams for the Shanty,

July:
5 was carpentering

6 was carpentering

7 Johannes and I picked out lumber

8 We were carpentering,

19 We did some building, all four of us, Alexander, Jonas Petter, Johannes and I on the Shanty.

20 the German Fischer brought some spirits to me, for 75 cents,

21	Johannes and I put a roof on my Shanty.
23	I stripped Bark for the shanty
24	I made a door for my Shanty,
28	I made hay on Nilsson's claim, Dug a Well

August:

9	Cut an opening for the door.
10	I put Doors in the doorway,
20	I cut lumber for my cattle shed.
26	I finished cutting lumber for my cattle shed
27	I was at Johannes' and worked on the cattle shed.
30	I laid the foundation for my cattle shed, Jonas Petter has altered a Coat for me, I'll work one day for him in payment,

December:

8	I began making the Table.
10	I finished the Table, I Nailed the moulding on the door of the cattle shed, fixed the Manger.
20	I did all sorts of Small chores.
23	I put the runners on the Sleigh.
25	Christmas Day.
26	we had choir practice and a meeting.
27 and 28	I patched up some of my old clothes.

1856

March:

11	last night we went fishing and got a boatload
27	I planted corn
28	we began gathering lumber for the church.
29	I worked at the church.
30	Ditto.

April:

| 13 | we dug the basement, My heifer has taken the Bull today. |
| 14 | I worked alone at the church and completed the door. |

June:

| 7 | I planted Corn and potatoes all day. |
| 8 | in the morning I dug Cabbage Beds and planted Red Beets, carrots, melons and Beans. |

21   I worked at the church, Put moulding on the windows

July:

9   this morning we have had an unusually strong and big Rain.

13   I hoed potatoes all day.

August:

21   cut wheat, among other things.

22   Sunday.

23   I was in Scandia and made a Casket for Peter Swensson and in the evening we buried him.

25   I was with Elsa at the Swedish Settlement at Caraoni [?, word unclear].

September:

2   I put up hay.

24   I was at a meeting all day, we had Baptisms, August Jonson and his wife were Baptized.

25   I harvested Corn all day and Completed it.

1858

February:

26   Sold 29 pounds of pork for 2 cents a pound

March:

13   Bought Canadian wheat as seed for 1 dollar and 50 cents per bushel

18   The ground has thawed everywhere Big thunder storm with heavy rain, unusual for this time of year in Minnesota

27   Bought a sack of meal. The meal cost 5 dollars a barrel. Paid too much money for freighting it. (greedy dogs!)

May:

1   planted seedlings all day

27   Sold potatoes at 25 cents per bushel. Made 4,750 shingles.

June:

3   Picked caterpillers [*sic*] off the seedlings, paid 86 dollars in taxes to the assessor Spent a lot of time with him

July:

           Paid 37 dollars in taxes

September:

  17   Sowed and harrowed the fall wheat

  25   Finished cutting the corn

October:

  19   In Saint Paul and traded the big oxen for a couple of smaller ones.

  25   Borrowed a harvester, Harvested 25 bushels of rye and 7½ bushels of wheat

November:

   8   Planted plum trees

  18   sold wheat for 1.25 per bushel

  19   made coops for the hens

  22   butchered a hog that weighed 212 pounds, he had 14 pounds of lard

December:

  20   made a bed

1859

January:

   3   was at a party at Mr. Nilsson's and had spiritual Conversations.

   5   the Sow has taken the Boar today for the second time.

   6   large amounts of Snow have fallen today.

   7   Began smoking the pork.

   8   did nothing, was not well, bought a pint of wine in a bottle for 80 ct.

1862

April:

  10   split Fence Slats, in the evening we had a meeting at missis Månsson's and prayers for our newborn Children.

  12   we had a school meeting in the schoolhouse.

  13   I bought cowbells and hung them on the calves.

  14   took the heifer Lady to Nilsson's Bull.

  16   I bought an iron harrow for 2 dollars 5 ct.

21   today the other young Lamb had a lamb, and it was a ram.

April.

25   I have had to kill the heifer Fröken, she calved yesterday. I have boiled over a gallon of Syrup today, this evening we had a meeting at our place.

27   I dressed hens. Mäbba has taken the Bull today.

30   today is penance and prayer day, Elsa is at a meeting, sowed oats and harrowed.

December

15   we cleared a path along the Line between Jonas Petter and my place.

16   Johannes Axsell, a boy, was born at 12:30 this morning. I have done all sorts of Small chores today.

20   in the evening I took the Hides over to Johannes that the Dalecarlians are going to prepare.

25   Christmas Day, we were at church services all day.

27   I mended Old shoes.

31   I hauled corn and straw, among other things.

1870

October:

3, 4, 5   did work on the new House.

6   this evening we had to Butcher the cow Betty, since she had eaten too much Rapeseed

8   put in doors in the House. I cut Up and Salted the Meat and went to Waconia and sold the Cow-hide, got 4 dollars.

14   we moved into our new house in the morning, in the evening we were at Nicklas Swenson's place for a Wedding (Carna was the bride).

15, 16, 17 I did all sorts of Small chores, Lars hauled Manure, in the evenings we had services

24   general prayer and Thanksgiving Day, and we have had a religious service.

26   I fixed all kinds of things in the cow shed, Elsa and the children have threshed corn. This week

it has been warm and rather beautiful weather, and we still haven't had any snow.

27   Sunday.

28   I did repairs around the cow shed, Elsa threshed corn.

December:

1   I painted the cow sheds.

3   I took 18 bushels of Rye to the Waconia mill, came home with Runners for the sleigh.

5   I made a Shed for firewood.

6   I did all sorts of Small chores.

7   I went to Per Danjel's and Butchered.

12   Elsa and I went to Andrew Swan's for a Funeral, his Son Henry was buried.

13   I took the Black spotted Sow to Simon's boar.

14   We butchered one of the large boars and a pig, I got Per Danjell to help me.

18   Sunday.

19   The heifer Lady calved last night.

1881

March:

29   we cut and hauled oak Logs,

30   we hauled Logs, among other things but I injured my Back Lifting So I could hardly walk home.

31   I am in bed with a Backache, The boys are busy with the farm animals.

April:

1   I am still in Bed with a Backache,

2   this morning I did small tasks, in the evening we had an extra school meeting.

5   repaired Shoes in the morning, went to Waconia in the evening.

8   I wrote a letter to Sweden and Mailed it As well as a letter to my Brother-in-law John Anderson, the black-spotted Sow had Pigs.

9   The boys are hauling Manure and cleaning out the sheep pen, I repaired Shoes.

18   We began boring the Maple trees today,

A Swedish Farmer

19	we bored the Maples,
20	Same thing,
21	we began Sowing wheat.
22	we had a church meeting
30	yesterday we sheared the sheep

1898

March:

12   last night we got 3 inches of Snow, this morning Frank and Josefina went down to minneapolis. I did Small chores.

16   The boys Hammered on the Last boards for the Barn. I did nothing I am not well. There's a heavy Storm today.

18   Frank hauled milk to Waconia, in the evening we got a lot of Snow.

21   The boys Bored the Maple trees, laid brick for the ovens, etc.—I was in Bed, I am not well—fine weather.

22   it is very cold today with a northerly wind, I was in Bed

23   Frank and Axsell did this and that, I am not well.

24   Frank was at Peterman's, Axsell did small jobs. In the evening Sven Svenson and his wife Ingri Stina and Beata Carlson were here on a visit, I was in Bed, Dry and beautiful weather.

25   The boys collected Maple Sap and did small jobs.

26   Frank hauled milk and Maple Sap and began Sowing wheat in the home field—I got so Sick today That they had to carry me to Bed.

27   Sunday, it snowed all day today,

28   Frank was in Waconia with a load of wheat, in the evening the boys hauled manure—It is now fit for full Sledding, I am not well.

29   The boys hauled manure—I was in Bed, it is clear weather but not mild weather.

[Two days later, on the 31st of March, 1898, Andrew Peterson passed away on his farm near Waconia in Carver County, Minnesota.]

CHAPTER 3

A Swedish Cemetery in America

One of the most typical Swedish settlements in the Midwest—
and very probably in the whole United States—is Chisago County,
an area in eastern Minnesota, where the St. Croix River forms
the border with Wisconsin. The word *Chisago* comes from the
Chippewa language and is said to mean "beautiful land." It was
the Chippewa tribe, in other words, that once owned this beautiful land. From the 1850s onward, the area was a place of settlement for emigrant Smålanders. This land, where a hundred
years ago the Indians set up their huts and lit their campfires,
has become a bit of Kronoberg County,[1] transplanted to the fertile
soil of Minnesota.

The very first Swedes on this spot, however, were from Hälsingland and Östergötland. In the year 1854 the first Evangelical
Lutheran congregation was organized by the new immigrants
in present-day Center City in Chisago County, and today this
congregation's oldest membership list supplies us with details
about the first immigrants' names and places of birth in Sweden:
in 1850 Per Andersson, Daniel Rättig, L. P. Sjölin, and Per Berg,
all with their families, arrived from Hassela in Hälsingland. At
the same time the families of Anders Svensson and L. J. Stark
came from Kettilstad in Östergötland. Two years later came the
first Smålanders; in 1852 thirteen people whose names are given
in the church book arrived from Kronoberg County. Seven of
them brought their families; in one case there were nine children

56

in the family, all of whom accompanied their parents across the Atlantic. In the year 1853 came the first large contingent of Smålanders, sixty-four people, mostly family groups, and the following year there arrived another hundred or so, for whom parishes in Kronoberg County are given in the church book as their place of birth. In addition, twenty-odd persons are noted as coming from Kristianstad County and Blekinge. The figures in the congregation book give us an idea of the wide extent of family emigration.[2]

The immigrants traveled by steamboat up the St. Croix River. The landing places were in some cases Franconia, in others Taylors Falls;[3] today both of these places are beautiful and well-built communities. One hundred years ago the banks of the river were, of course, completely uninhabited. Further penetration up the St. Croix River was prevented by the swift rapids at Taylors Falls.

The oral tradition in Taylors Falls tells of four families from Småland who lived in isolation deep in this wilderness for several years before their settlement began to grow. One of the first houses that the settlers built here is still standing. It is ten feet square and eight feet from floor to ceiling. The house is built out of round logs. It is said that the cabin served as a home for fifteen people during the first year after their immigration.[4]

Most of the immigrants settled around Chisago Lake—a long string of connected lakes—and the colony grew so rapidly that as early as 1855 the number of inhabitants is reported to have been five hundred. Nevertheless, cholera ran rampant among the settlers, especially in the year 1854. A good many immigrants, who had been stricken with the illness during the journey, died soon after arriving at their destination. On the beautiful, shady banks of the St. Croix River at Franconia a place was pointed out to me where over fifty cholera victims are said to have been buried in a common grave. Rumors of this event are said to have reached the victims' hometown and frightened prospective emigrants away from traveling to America. At any rate, immigration to that area of Minnesota was less extensive during the years that followed immediately after 1854.

Thus it is descendants of these farmers from Hälsingland, Östergötland, Blekinge, Skåne and, above all, Småland who make their home in Chisago County today. During my stay in the area, I visited and became acquainted with all those small towns and communities where Swedish descendants are predominant: Chisago City, Lindstrom, Center City, Almelund, Franconia, Scandia, and other places. Here one can still hear the genuine old Småland dialect spoken—by great grandchildren of the first immigrants, who have very vague conceptions of their fore-fathers' home parishes. A few years ago there were still road signs written in Swedish at the road crossings here. At times—as when one meets somebody who speaks old-fashioned Små-landish—one has a strong sensation of being back home again, and then one thinks that any of these places could just as easily be called Tingsryd, Ljungby, or Lessebo.[5]

The area gives an impression of fertility and well-being. It is obvious that it pays to run a farm here. Minnesota's farmland consists of black humus and is rich in important mineral salts. The countryside shows similarities to the most fertile districts of Småland, such as the parishes around lakes Salen and Åsnen in Kronoberg County or certain parts of southern Kalmar County:[6] beautiful, level fields alternating with groves of deciduous trees and here and there the glitter of water from the bays of the lakes. The foliage is more luxuriant, however, than any place there at home. A hundred years ago there were wide expanses of pine forests here, now almost completely logged over without any replanting, and huge forests of oak then spread across the fields that are now farmland. The land is practically free of rocks[7]—a rock is a rarity in this part of Minnesota—but the cultivators had to struggle with the tree stumps instead; the roots of the huge oak trees must certainly have cost the settlers heavy labor. No one can look out over these vast fields of grain without admiring the work that was accomplished here by the first immigrants.

A Swedish Cemetery

And what more do we know about those who immigrated here from the farm districts of Sweden and cultivated the Chippewa Indians' beautiful land? We meet their descendants here, and many of them still plow the fields that their fathers or grandfathers farmed. But the latter we no longer meet. If we wish to look for the first people who came here, we have to go to the cemeteries: their names are written on the gravestones there.

Around the old settlement at Chisago Lake, there are many church cemeteries; every religious denomination has its own. Using the expression "churchyards" [kyrkogårdar] about burial places in America is somehow inappropriate, since they are never located adjacent to the churches but off to themselves in the fields and woods. And all the burial places I have seen over there have had settings of great natural beauty: in groves and leafy copses, near the banks of a lake, on hills that are shaded by tall broadleaf trees. The resting place for the dead is chosen with care in America.[8]

Now my task in this place was also to seek out the dead; I inquired about the oldest cemetery thereabouts and found it at last. The spot obviously is beginning to be forgotten: my guide, who was himself born in the area, had to stop and go into a couple of houses and ask for directions before he could find his way there. Not far from Chisago City, on the banks of Chisago Lake, lies the oldest graveyard in Chisago County; at the same time it is one of the oldest cemeteries in Minnesota. The lake down below has steep banks, and the graveyard is located on the slope of a hill that is formed by the banks. It has no fence and at first glance can hardly be distinguished from the surrounding fields.[9]

I arrived at this spot one evening in the midst of the harvest season; in one of the adjacent fields a tractor with a binder passed by; in another field a dense stand of wheat shocks was arrayed. The spot is separated from the lake by a high, green wall of stately, shady maples and elms.

Concerning the sight of the old cemetery there on the headland by the banks of Chisago Lake, I feel I have to use an expression that is somewhat trite but difficult to replace: an experience.

In the church records at home I have gone through the names of the parishioners after whom it is noted: "Emigrated to N. America."[10] This entry appears at the top of each page; thereafter it says "Ditto," from the top all the way down only this, "Ditto." On the gravestones here I found several of these names again. And once again there is the question of making a move. But this time it is a question of each person's final journey: from the land of the living to the land of the dead. I am standing on the spot that was the final and conclusive destination here in this world for those who once took out a visa to emigrate from their home parish: here I have found their graves.

In most cases the place of birth for the person who rests below is given on the tombstone: "born in Algutsboda, Sweden," "born in Långasjö, Sweden," "born in Linneryd, Sweden," "born in Elmeboda, Sweden." These stones gave me a unique sensation; out here, so far from home, in another part of the world, lies grave after grave with those well-known parish names. It seemed to me as if Konga and Uppvidinge townships in Kronoberg County had joined together in establishing a graveyard for their lost sons and daughters here in America. Here, in the middle of this huge foreign land, suddenly lies before me a small bit of another country. This headland, located near the lake with the Chippewa name, is a bit of Småland. This is a Swedish cemetery in America.

The names of those who are buried here are our most common ones in Sweden, sometimes with slightly altered spelling: Carlson, Johanson, Nelson, Peterson, Johnson. The old Swedish soldiers' names are also represented: Lans, Lif, Kron, Rolig, Frost, Strand, Glad, Bäck.[11] The soldiers' cottages in the Småland of the 1850s and 1860s were full of children; it was said you could not open a window or a door without a child tumbling out. Here I can now verify with my own eyes that many of those who were born in the soldiers' cottages back home emigrated

A Swedish Cemetery

to Chisago County in Minnesota and found their final resting place on the shores of Chisago Lake.

With their expressively laconic inscriptions, these tombstones tell the history of Swedish emigration. The birthdates of the deceased supply us with essential details. Here is buried a Swedish immigrant who was born as early as the eighteenth century: Jonas P. Falk, born on the 17th of September, 1793, died on the 15th of November, 1881. That is the oldest date of birth I can find here; no place of birth in Sweden is given, nor is the year of his arrival here. But it is now the opinion that no Swede—except for Fahlström, mentioned in chapter 1—was in this part of Minnesota before 1850; thus Falk must have been over fifty years of age when he emigrated. And on several graves appear birthdates from the first decade of the nineteenth century. In other words, a good many of the emigrants from the first years had already reached middle age at the time of their emigration to America, a fact that we have hardly paid any attention to at home and that was news to me, at any rate. There have to be compelling reasons when a person emigrates at an age when the prime of his life is drawing to a close and the transplantation to a new environment must pose special difficulties.

On almost every tombstone a biblical proverb is written or a couple of lines from a verse in *Svenska psalmboken* [The Swedish hymnal] are inscribed. The Swedish is archaic: "I skolen ingå i Hans Rolighet" [You shall rest in His peace]; "Allt härintills hafwer Herren hulpet" [The Lord has helped in everything up to now].[12] This language, with its echo of old country churches from nineteenth-century Sweden, strikes a note of contrast in these surroundings—in this country where mechanization has been carried to its extreme and where modern technology, in all its manifestations, rules supreme: old Lutheran farming communities in Småland, with their churches on the hill and their horses and buggies, here meet the vast America of our day that contains forty million automobiles within its borders.

The spelling of the words on some of the gravestones completes the picture of a graveyard for Swedish commoners: "Her

61

hwilar vor modar" [Here rests our mother]; "I ären gångna till ett herrligt Land" [You have gone to a wondrous land]; "Wi mötas åtar" [We shall meet again]. We can see the man who inscribed these lines on the stone, a man unaccustomed to the written word, who with an awkward and uncertain hand used the Swedish language and spelled the words to the best of his ability, as well as he remembered them after so many years in this foreign country.

In some places the Swedish has taken its form from the language of the new homeland, as, for example, in the expression *hustru af* [wife of].[13] Otherwise it should be pointed out that the inscriptions on the gravestones are remarkably unaffected by English; for the generation of Swedes who are buried in this cemetery, their mother tongue was still the language of everyday life.

The wild grass grows high around the stones, and in several places their inscriptions are so weathered or so overgrown with moss that the words are illegible nowadays. Time has taken its toll; this, the resting place of the dead, is old and half-forgotten, and it has been a long time since anyone was buried here. I scrape away at a small stone on the edge of the cemetery, right next to the field of wheat shocks, and make out a few words: "Lena Stina, born in Algutsboda, Sweden." The stone has begun to crumble, and the rest of the inscription is illegible. I can only make out the first name of the deceased. Here I would very much have liked to read more—she who is buried here is in fact my grandmother's sister. And something else has obviously been written here on the stone; here are traces of worn-off words. But I have to be satisfied with the paltry words that I can read about the deceased; about "Lena Stina, born in Algutsboda," I know somewhat more than what this tombstone reveals, but not much more. I know that my grandmother's oldest sister was a young widow, who sometime around the middle of the previous century emigrated to North America with five young children. Died in 1861—she passed away in the prime of life. A lone woman who journeyed to the wilderness of Minnesota with all of her

A Swedish Cemetery

small ones—a resolute woman. I feel that I know her through
my grandmother, who also suffered through many vicissitudes,
but who was astonishingly tough. I recall that she mentioned
her sister Inga-Lena[14] as a stubborn, almost incorrigible person,
who absolutely insisted on getting her own way. With those
words my grandmother also characterized herself . . .

Inga-Lena has now been forgotten in her home parish for
nearly a hundred years. And here on this headland next to the
glittering waters of Chisago Lake she has returned to the dust
again. "Måtte Jag Roligt Sofwa" [May I rest in Peace] it says on
her stone. And completely unintentionally I move very slowly
and quietly, when I leave there, as if I had come close to disturbing Inga-Lena's repose—I, a stranger from far away and yet
a relative from home.

So I wander around in the cemetery at Chisago Lake and try
to decipher the riddles that are contained in the mouldered inscriptions on the tombstones. And I reflect that there are many
other cemeteries in America that conceal the remains of people
from home. I think of the nameless graves on the shore of the
St. Croix River; those who were laid to rest on those banks
emigrated to America in order to die. They made a long and
arduous journey before they reached their graves. And I think
of all those thousands of my fellow countrymen who quite simply
disappeared and quietly succumbed in this vast country. I remember relatives who left and never came back; I remember
friends from my childhood and youth about whose fate in America little is known, about whose deaths no one knows anything,
and whose graves no one is aware of.[15] I think of those who
never wrote home to tell of the setbacks in their lives over here,
but remained silent and died. In America one is constantly amazed
at everything that the Swedes have managed to accomplish in
this country. In some communities one is reminded of their deeds
at every step. We have great victories to recall in America. But
it should also be remembered that this great Swedish contribution has taken its toll of human lives. In this country Swedes
have more graves than in any other country on earth outside

their own—and certainly more forgotten graves than in any other land. And we know so little about how the great majority of these kinsmen of ours lived; we know so little about how they died. The letters from America, which were so easy to recognize because of their long, white envelopes, just quit coming one day. The rest is silence.

This summer evening near the little lake is mild, like all summer evenings in Minnesota. From the field that lies next to the cemetery comes the roar of a tractor. Majestically the binding machine passes through the grain, and the sheaves fall behind the machine close, close together, in long, endless rows. This is the wheat that is being harvested, and here on these vast, flat fields a bounteous crop is being gathered in: the shocks rise in immense numbers as far as the eye can see across Chisago County. Minnesota is one of the breadbaskets of the United States. From here comes part of the bread that is sent to the starving in the Old World, where the nations have devastated themselves in two great civil wars. Old Mother Europe starves—and young America hastens to the rescue.

But the people who worked these fields from the beginning have mouldered in their graves here on this headland; they lie here as close to their old fields as they could get. They came here bringing with them their poverty—and nothing more. They were no heroes bearing sword and shield and coats of mail; they were merely common folk in gray homespun clothes who wore the wooden shoes that they themselves had made. Their story is little known in the country that bore them, and above them grows the wild grass of oblivion. Now tombstones with epitaphs in another language have been raised over their deceased descendants. And soon no one will any longer be able to make out what is written on the tombstones of the first immigrants—not only because it is disappearing and crumbling away but also because the words are inscribed on the stone in an unintelligible and forgotten language—a language that has become foreign to the tongues of their own descendants.

A Swedish Cemetery

But as long as the fields hereabout are still being plowed and their growing grain is still being cut, their *achievements* will remain to tell of them—of these men and women in homespun and wooden shoes who came from the poor farm districts of Sweden, of the men and women who came from a small country in a far-off corner of the world, of this folk from rock-strewn Småland who came here and tilled the soil in the Chippewa Indians' great, wild land.

CHAPTER 4

"A newspaper with Swedish type . . ."

The Swedish-language press in America, which nowadays consists of only around thirty papers (in 1968—only seven papers), will be able to celebrate its one-hundredth anniversary in a few years. The first fumbling attempt to put out a newspaper in the United States for emigrants from Sweden was made in the year 1851; a weekly named *Skandinaven* [The Scandinavian] appeared for a short time in New York. This publication was printed in Swedish, but as the name indicates it was intended for readers from all the Scandinavian countries. *Skandinaven* folded before it was one year old.[1]

The first Swedish-language newspaper in the United States of America, published exclusively for our countrymen among the pioneers, was *Den Swenska Posten* [The Swedish post], which began publication in the year 1854 in Galesburg, Illinois. During my stay in the small town of Lindstrom, Minnesota, I had the opportunity to study the first editions of this paper, which are preserved in the home of the Norelius brothers, descendants of the publisher.[2] During my life I have seldom come across any more interesting reading material. These old editions of the newspaper are irreplaceable documents that tell us a good deal about the lives of our countrymen in America. But apart from that, a person is captivated by the picture that these old yellowed pages convey of a Swedish newspaper pioneer in North America and his multifarious hardships and difficulties. One might guess beforehand that putting out a newspaper for pioneers was a delicate and special business, but not until one has read through a couple of years' editions of this first periodical publication in our language in America does one really begin to realize how difficult this business was.

A Swedish minister, T. N. Hasselquist, was called as the pastor to the newly founded Lutheran congregation in Galesburg in 1852.[3] Hasselquist had his origins in Osby in Skåne. He had not been at work among his fellow countrymen in Illinois for very long before he realized that they were without a spokesman— that a newspaper was needed for these colonists. And on the 1st of October, 1854, the first edition of *Den Swenska Posten* came out in Galesburg in Knox County, Illinois. It introduces itself as "the only Swedish newspaper in America" and its publisher is "The Reverend T. N. Hasselquist."

Pastor Hasselquist writes a rather lengthy "Notice" in this edition and announces that his newspaper will be published every two weeks and will cost one dollar a year "in advance." It will contain two sections, one political, the other ecclesiastical. In addition, the editor explains that he will introduce into the political section, on the one hand, "as many selected items from the old country as can be obtained by way of newspapers and letters," on the other hand, "the most notable events that take place in our new homeland, which it may be necessary to know about." In reference to the recent outbreak of the Crimean War— the major world event in the fall of 1854[4]—he adds, among other things:

"Most of us cannot so easily dispel all our thoughts of, and love for, our home communities to the extent that we do not wish to follow everything that happens there with lively interest. There is no denying that the war, doubtless to be protracted, which has begun in Europe and which is certain to become widespread, will bring with it great changes, whereof our mother country will also pay a price. One can liken Sweden's position in this war to a small boat between two large vessels; when the latter two collide the former is in great danger of being crushed." It is noted that public opinion in Sweden is hostile to Russia— "for long-standing and natural reasons."[5] The editor also promises that his newspaper will contain "the most common items concerning the railroads, farming, and agricultural economy, as well as details on the prices of different kinds of grain in the bigger cities."

When a person has read to the end of this "Notice," he is rather surprised: with that he has read the whole newspaper! It turns out that this edition of the newspaper consists of nothing more than the editor's "Notice." It is 35 × 25 centimeters in format and is printed on only one side of the paper. One finds the explanation for these rather one-sided contents in a small item in one corner at the bottom of the page under the heading "A Comment": "Our intent was to get the entire first edition printed in the size the paper should have in the future, but when, after much fuss, everything was ready and the setting of type had gone on a bit it was discovered that an adequate supply of the letter *k* was missing, due to the fact that so few *k*s are used in English; this is the reason that only the 'Notice' could be printed. This was rather annoying to me.

"My desire now is that all of those who wish to read a Swedish newspaper will hasten to send in their order to *Den Swenska Posten* and preferably with 50 cents overpayment, *in order to ensure that the printing of a newspaper with Swedish type throughout will be able to take place.*"

We understand the editor's feelings in the face of this misfortune and are touched by his modest term for it: "rather annoying." Things certainly began badly for this new newspaper enterprise. Most likely this first edition of the paper, containing only a subscription notice, is perfectly unique in the history of the Swedish press.

But Reverend Hasselquist does not let his spirits sag because of the rough sledding at the outset. The newspaper continues to appear and as time goes by it takes on a more normal appearance: it is soon being printed in "the size the paper should have in the future." The first editions contain a great deal of important news from Sweden: fellow countrymen in America learn that obligatory church attendance in the old country "at long last has been abolished," that work on a telegraph line between Stockholm and Gothenburg has been completed, and that "railroads have begun to be considered."[6]

But one article, "The General Situation in America," is of special interest to a reader who picks up the newspaper one hundred years after the date of publication. Pastor Hasselquist mentions here that he has now resided in North America for three years and that after this length of time he considers himself ready to make a judgment about the new country. He writes, among other things:

"It cannot be denied that the United States, our new home, is a strange and highly remarkable country. Here there is almost nothing but the most blatant contrasts. Uprightness and honesty alongside the utmost degree of fraudulence and rapacity. Brotherly love and respect for others—and the most fierce bloodthirstiness. Many times it takes no more than a word before knives start flashing or revolvers go off. Democratic equality and the most aristocratic arrogance. The most highminded freedom—and, on the other hand, the most degrading slavery."

One can still agree with the author when he uses the expression "a highly remarkable country" to describe the United States. And what he writes with drastic simplification about the contrasts and the extremes still applies in our own time—even if to a lesser extent—to "the situation in America."

The monetary system in the North American Republic was still rather unsettled a hundred years ago. A striking testimony to this comes to us in editor Hasselquist's newspaper, where we read that great uncertainty exists "in respect to the different types of bills that are being distributed here." The newspaper promises information on all counterfeit or useless bank notes, "to the extent that they come to the attention of the editors." The paper also promises to publish the names of all the banks "that are considered to be totally defunct," so that the readers will be expressly notified and warned about these institutions. And the number of banks on the brink of ruin at that time was so great that one edition of *Den Swenska Posten* fills a whole column with a list of them! The publisher himself is so fundamentally suspicious of all paper money that he explains that he prefers that payments for the newspaper be sent to him in gold. "Bank Frauds" is a standing headline in his newspaper: "Under this title we shall list those banks that are reported to have been started solely in order to commit fraud."

The great, predominant problem in the United States at that time, the question of the abolition of Negro slavery, is often dealt with in the paper, and the publisher, naturally, takes the right side. He writes at one point: "Christianity and slavery are, however, the opposites of each other." And he shows a prophetic flair when he predicts that the slave question will cause a bloody civil war in America within a short time.[7]

In January of 1855, the newspaper changed its name to *Hemlandet, det Gamla och det Nya* [Homeland, the old and the new], and it was known by this name through its continued years of existence. The number of subscribers had by then grown to the respectable figure of 550, and in the month of March, 1855, the publisher reports with "an inner joy that subscriptions to the newspaper have become so widespread that its existence has been made secure, at least to begin with." A few readers have written to say that the subscription fee is too high, but editor Hasselquist carries openness and honesty with his readers so far that he reports in the newspaper all the costs of its publication. Which is probably also something unique in the history of the press. He has furthermore begun to accept advertisements at a price of five cents a line. He does not curry favor with his advertisers, however: "But only a few advertisements will be accepted," he writes—an announcement that a person does not often see in the newspapers.

When *Hemlandet, det Gamla och det Nya* finally developed a personality of its own, a person would have to describe the newspaper as a religious tract to as great an extent as it was a news organ. The church section gains more and more ground on the political one and claims an ever larger amount of space. Pastor Hasselquist energetically defends the purity of the Lutheran faith and has hardly a word to spare for other religious views. It is especially noticeable that his intolerance toward Methodists and Baptists is as complete as it could possibly be; these teachings are described as "un-American in their spirit and aims" and as being "dangerous enemies of the Republic." But he most severely condemns the Mormons, who at that time obviously shocked public opinion in America with their "ungodly polygamy." About their high priest we learn: "He is reported to have a total of 50 to 60 wives, and many others have just as many in proportion. A few years ago one of the Swedes from here traveled through Utah on his way to California and saw the high priest leading the way for 28 wives, most of whom carried children in their arms. Since no agreement exists between all of these women when they are in a house, the men have of late begun to build a room for every wife off to the side of the actual house. When a new wife is taken, a new room is built."

Hemlandet's principal area of distribution was Illinois and Minnesota, which latter area did not receive the honor of being a state in the Union until 1858. In the beginning of the 1850s, Minnesota Territory was still practically a wilderness. Inside an area nearly the same size as the kingdom of Sweden there lived only 150,000 people. But during these years the great in-migration had gotten started; the settlers from northern Europe had come. *Hemlandet* tells about the colonization in a news item:

"The Norwegians and the Swedes are beginning to swarm in like bees in some parts of the Territory. Emigrants are arriving in such great and overwhelming numbers this year that the poor people cannot find decent dwellings, but lodge out in the woods and fields like animals. Some are forced to build shacks for themselves out of earth and stakes, in the absence of sawed logs on many of the prairies where they settle.

71

"These Scandinavians who are arriving are, in general, a diligent and honest folk. Although they have peculiarities in their manners, the Americans look on them with much goodwill and consider them to be the very best class of emigrated foreigners."

From the Swedish settlements in Illinois as well as Minnesota accounts of conditions among the colonists regularly flow in to the newspaper. From these it is evident that extreme poverty exists in many places; some of the immigrant families are completely destitute. Many of the newcomers have put themselves in debt for the trip from Sweden. But those who have lived in America for a while, for one or two years, have already begun to improve their conditions, and it is said that their lot is not at all bad. And hunting and fishing are lifesavers for the settler when all other food runs low on his table.

A colony that has made great headway in a surprisingly short time, according to *Hemlandet,* is at Chisago Lake, the Smålanders' settlement in Chisago County. In only four years its population has increased from four families to more than five hundred people, and during the same period the colonists' total holdings have grown from almost nothing at all to a value of nearly 20,000 dollars.[8]

Periodically the newspaper's publisher takes long journeys through the Swedish settlement areas roundabout the Midwest, and the observations from these trips, which he publishes in *Hemlandet,* from the viewpoint of posterity comprise the most valuable parts of its contents. His reports from these settlements, with all their genuine and graphic portrayals, provide an indispensable documentary contribution to the history of our fellow countrymen's settlements in North America.

The Reverend Hasselquist's newspaper advocates temperance and opposes the existence of taverns, which exploit his fellow countrymen's weakness for strong drink. Even the use of tobacco is condemned, but when the newspaper also begins to turn against snuff, the editor's desk is flooded with letters from indignant readers. As convincing proof of the blessed effects of snuff, one reader testifies that he knew an old woman who used a pound of snuff a week and reached the age of ninety.

No matter how dearly the editor loves temperance and eagerly supports its success, he reacts against the proceedings within certain secret societies that use "signs and robes of their orders." We are also informed of a shocking example of the shady things that can occur in those quarters: "Many such societies, out of an exaggerated zeal for temperance, have long used a mixture of water, vinegar, and syrup instead of wine when taking communion and have thereby broken God's commandment and the rules of Christ with their regulations."

The newspaper constantly has difficulties with its printing and publication and, above all, there is a shortage of "Swedish letters." New Swedish type has been ordered, but in February of 1855 it still has not arrived. Until further notice, the paper must therefore be printed at an American printing house, which costs the publisher nearly twice what was expected. Because of the high printing costs only one issue a month is brought out— "until the greatly longed-for Swedish type gets here." Later the editor himself makes a trip to Chicago in order to pick up printer's paper, which he had purchased "but which could not be delivered here by freight train."

Despite all his hardships as the publisher of a frontier newspaper, Pastor Hasselquist finds time for his own more private business enterprises, such as, for example, the selling of certain splendid medicines. He announces, among other things, that he offers for sale a newly discovered, effective remedy for the ague, which will be sent to all Swedish settlements in the area as soon as he has been able to get reliable men as agents. One batch of this remedy, two bottles, costs one dollar and seventy-five cents. He even functions in the newspaper as an adviser to readers on their more intimate and personal affairs. Thus he starts a column in his newspaper that could be described as a forerunner of the "Dear Helena" column in *Dagens Nyheter*. At one point he warns young unmarried Swedish women about getting married "to bad people from both Sweden and America." There had been cases in the Swedish settlements, you see, when young girls had gotten married to men who happened completely to forget that they also had wives in Sweden. But no matter how false and treacherous the Swedish men may be, the Americans are obviously not any angels in trousers either. Even when a girl is going to get married to an American, there exists a certain danger that the bridegroom may be a scoundrel. Pastor Hasselquist especially brings home to the young women the fact that they should not pay any attention to a man's outward appearance: "Don't look at his fine coat and hat or his polite manners, for the worst scoundrel may be lurking just underneath."

As fillers, short expressive maxims and tales with a moral to them sometimes appear in the newspaper. Thus we read about an effective remedy for swearing; one foresighted mother, who wished to break her son of the habit of cursing, washed his mouth out with strong lye soap every time he had said a swear word. The cure took effect after two weeks. And a truly memorable idea is contained in the following maxim: "The best and most proper way to come into wealth is obviously to seek it down the path of hard work alone, but in that connection don't forget *prayer either*.

The newspaper's successes continue. By August of 1855, the number of subscribers has increased to 729 and by the end of the year the figure is up to 800. The format has been enlarged and now has four pages and five columns per page, and the newspaper comes out every fourteenth day, just as it originally did. The last edition of the year is mailed out in duplicate copies to all subscribers, who are urged to lend it to their neighbors and they in turn to their neighbors, "so that no one may be in ignorance of the fact that even the Swedes have their own newspaper in America."

And in the final edition of the year editor Hasselquist writes: "To begin with I was completely unaccustomed to all the writing that a newspaper publisher has to do, along with other duties connected with the job. Now I am somewhat practiced in the duties of an editor."

Pastor Hasselquist is also a prominent figure in the history of the Swedish church in America, but this branch of his activities lies outside the subject of our article. His newspaper *Hemlandet, det Gamla och det Nya* proved, however, to be a permanent enterprise and became one of the foremost voices of the Swedish-American press. The newspaper continued to be published for all of sixty years, all the way up to 1914, when it merged with *Svenska Tribunen Nyheter* [The Swedish tribune news]—and during this whole time it was printed "with Swedish type throughout."

CHAPTER 5

The Pioneers' Church

When I lived in the small town of Monterey, California, I passed by a Baptist church at some time or other every day. Outside the church stood a brown-painted wooden bench that carried the following words in elegant, white letters on the back:

Sit down, neighbor, and rest.
This church is a friendly church.

This self-characterization could apply to many other churches in the United States. In general, American churches are friendly; their clergymen take the same accommodating and inviting attitude toward the public as a businessman toward a prospective customer: everyone is regarded as a future member of the congregation. Every time I moved into a new house in a new town, the same story was repeated. A friendly, cultivated voice was to be heard on the telephone: "This is Pastor X from Congregation Y. We know that you are a newcomer in our town—could we maybe have the pleasure of seeing you at our church? At eight o'clock tomorrow evening, for example, we have . . ." After I had explained that unfortunately I probably could not promise them the pleasure they had counted on, a new question generally followed: "Could I already be a member of some other church?" Then followed a distinctly negative answer (I view my obligatory

76

The Pioneers' Church

membership in the Swedish State Church to a large degree as a formality),[1] but my explanation usually only instilled the friendly pastor at the other end of the line with new hope: "But under such circumstances it might just be possible that—yes, we'll be waiting for you . . .!"

Churches in America are equipped, in other words, with an effective intelligence service: they know of every newly arrived stranger in town and get hold of his telephone number. This form of advertising enterprise has yet to catch on with businessmen in America; at least I was never called up by any grocery store owner who was trying to recruit me as a customer. Of course even men of the cloth ought to be granted the right to utilize the advantages of modern advertising technology for their own purposes. But I am afraid that methods that are too pushy only work against their aim. Even friendliness can be so exaggerated that it is interpreted as the opposite by somewhat sensitive people. In regard to the needs of the human soul, an effective service can easily become repulsive and ineffective. Around 1930 during the Depression era in the United States, there are said to have appeared especially concise and short sermons intended for very busy businessmen—a spiritual quick lunch served up in the shortest possible time. Perhaps it provoked a stock market mogul here and there to reflect, but in principle people take a skeptical attitude toward all forms of quick spiritual edification. At times a person also feels a little annoyance in the presence of the blasphemous expressions contained in church advertisements in America. On the ceiling of a streetcar one might catch sight of an ad: *"Do you know the way to the kingdom of heaven? If not—call this number———."* And among all the glittering signs advertising movies, laxative tablets, and boxing matches, one can suddenly see the name of the man from Nazareth in bright crimson neon letters: "JESUS THE LIGHT OF THE WORLD." And from a Swedish-American newspaper, one of those with the widest circulation over there, I have cut out an expressive advertisement:

BIG WASH
If your sins are as red as blood, they can
become as white as snow. The blood of
Jesus, His Son, cleanses all sins.
REVIVAL MEETINGS
continue every evening at 8 o'clock in the
Temple, 213–221 East 52nd Street.

The heading of this advertisement caught my eye just as I was looking through the classified section of the newspaper for the address of a good and reliable Swedish laundry.

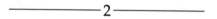

As everyone knows, the United States has no state church. The number of free churches is all the greater. As early as the year 1850 there existed no fewer than eighty-seven different religious denominations and sects within the North American republic. Since then, of course, this figure has increased many times over. In 1920 the Christian denominations alone amounted to sixty-eight, containing 234,330 congregations. There is probably no one who knows for certain how large the total number of religious sects—Christian, Mohammedan, Buddhist, Spiritualist, and so forth—is today. There is one report that there might be around six hundred.

In the United States Constitution the following is prescribed: *Congress shall make no law respecting an establishment of religion, or prohibiting the free exercise thereof.* With these words the principle of complete freedom of religion has been splendidly laid out in one short and concise sentence. And this principle has been practiced in the North American republic for nearly a hundred and fifty years.

Every individual gifted with normal intelligence naturally rejects all forms of state religion and demands complete freedom of religion. A state cannot believe anything; all religious belief must be solely the concern of the individual. Some time ago these headlines appeared in Swedish newspapers: "Unlimited right to leave the State Church suggested by committee," "Mon-asteries to be permitted according to proposal." Here in Sweden there still remains a good deal to be done before freedom of religion is completely established. In regard to religious toler-ance, our country is backward in comparison with America. The Swedish people still lack a freedom that the American people have enjoyed during nearly their entire history. Our ruling party—the Social Democrats—has taken a completely reactionary po-sition on this issue. The Kingdom of Sweden cannot very well believe anything, but nevertheless for nearly 450 years the state, on behalf of its patient and obedient inhabitants, has embraced the Evangelical Lutheran doctrine according to the Augsburg Confession.

It is necessary to consider the free church in America against its historical background:[2] it was founded by immigrants who had been subjected to religious persecution in the Old World. Even in Sweden, as has been mentioned before, intolerance by the authorities toward people holding different religious opin-ions was a factor that contributed to emigration before the year 1858. The Conventicle Decree, that unique document of 1726, forbade the members of the Swedish State Church to think for themselves. It encourages the king's subjects to "abstain from profound questions and doctrinal disputes, which are too deep for the simpleminded and could give cause for delusion." The document constitutes a blemish on the record of the Swedish church of the past, and the connection between the Conventicle Decree and emigration is a dark chapter in the history of the Swedish State Church that our clergymen do not generally talk about of their own volition. It is a strange irony of history that the archbishop of the Kingdom of Sweden visited the Swedish settlement areas of America in the summer of 1948 in order to participate in paying homage to those pioneers whom the Swed-ish State Church had driven into exile a hundred years earlier.[3]

In the New World now each immigrant could believe what he wished and worship whatever god he wished. As a natural result of this freedom, there arose a host of different churches and religious denominations. The realization of total religious freedom is bound to result in this type of religious confusion. There is much in America's church life that is objectionable. The unlimited tolerance of people with different religious opinions has given free play to the most peculiar ideas. No matter how ridiculous and absurd a doctrine has seemed, it has always won over some followers. It also stands to reason that out of two hundred million people there would be a good number of simpleminded and mentally disturbed individuals. These strange outcroppings on the tree of religion have caused a great deal of tumult, but in fact they have not had any great significance, and they cannot in any way be regarded as typical of church life in the United States. The spirit of free, private enterprise in religion in America can appear in repulsive forms and express itself in unsavory ways. But it is still definitely to be preferred to a government care of souls and state monopoly over the human soul.

Now it is completely natural that strong opposition has arisen between the six hundred religious denominations and sects that are active in the United States due to the complete freedom of religion. Harsh competition and rivalry have arisen between the churches; they are fighting over human souls. And it is from this point of view that we have to see the clergyman who calls up a recently arrived stranger in a town and says: "Perhaps we might have the pleasure of . . .?"

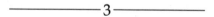

———————— 3 ————————

In the Swedish areas of the Midwest, a visiting foreigner immediately notices the dominant position that church life occupies. A person cannot rightly understand the great power and strong influence of the church if he does not bear in mind its historical conditions—from pioneer days.[4]

The first Swedish emigrants came from areas where the church was all-powerful in the spiritual domain and even had authority in the worldly sphere, and where the ministers represented an absolute authority among the common people.[5] The church on the hill was in all senses the focal point of the parish and its public meeting place. People met with friends and relatives there, and on Sundays even errands of a secular nature were carried out there. And when the farmers from these areas came to the prairies of Nebraska and the forests of Minnesota, they missed the parish church and the churchyard. Their first collective act was to build themselves a church. They felled trees and split logs for their new temple; they worked and toiled and outdid each other in the spirit of self-sacrifice. They organized small congregations everywhere: Lutheran, Presbyterian,[6] Methodist, Baptist, and so forth. The settlers wanted to hear God's word in their mother tongue; they wanted to have a place where they could meet. And through the building of a church they even satisfied their purely worldly needs. No one can help noticing the commercial features of church life in America; one notes it, for example, in the plain business terms that are used by ministers in their sermons. One can see announcements of this type: *"Deposit your money in the Bank of the Kingdom of Mercy! Best possible return!"* This linking up with the business world is a prominent feature of the pioneer church. In the temple the pioneers attended even to their purely worldly affairs, since it was their only meeting place. And in doing so, the immigrants who came from Swedish country churches were only following the customs of their homeland. In the old days farmers settled their business on the church grounds, and the pulpits were often used as a place to make announcements; from the pulpit farms were offered for sale; market days, livestock auctions, and property settlements were announced; times and places for the services of stallions and boars were given, and so forth. Examples of this type could be multiplied over and over.

It is obvious, in other words, that from its very beginning the church played a major role in the lives of the first emigrants and constituted an indispensable bond between them. For these settlers church life was the only form of cultural intercourse in the new country. Their temples were temples for free worship services; no worldly authorities meddled in their affairs. They had come to the land of liberty, they had brought their God with them, and they could freely profess their faith in him in any form they wished. One understands these defiant, indomitable farmers, and one has a liking for them.

But how has this church that the pioneers laid the foundation for developed during the past hundred years? It has been allowed to grow in complete freedom in America, undisturbed by any federal measures and intervention. What is remarkable and difficult to account for is that the church to a large extent remains in its beginning stages and to a great degree still retains the character of a pioneer church. In this connection I want to point out, however, that my observations mainly concern the rural areas and the smaller towns of the Midwest and Upper Midwest and that they are consequently of limited validity. But in these Swedish settlements the absence of what we call secular culture is immediately obvious to a foreigner: church life is still practically the only form of cultural intercourse between people.

I lived for a couple of months in a town of about fifteen thousand inhabitants in Michigan. Two institutions existed in this town in about equal numbers: churches and taverns. The town had sixteen places of worship and nineteen saloons. Here existed two strictly separate worlds: the worlds of the church and the tavern. Outside of them there appeared to me to be an absolute vacuum. And despite the existence of sixteen churches—several of them large and magnificent temples—this town gave me an impression of spiritual poverty. Now it is obviously not fair to make a comparison between a young pioneering community in the Upper Midwest and an old, cultured city of the same size in Sweden. But any visitor from Sweden who had come to this place would have missed the same things as I did: a theater, a concert hall, a public library reading room, an art gallery—all of those institutions where different forms of culture have their abode.

I explained these impressions of mine to many of the townspeople and members of the different churches. Several of them were my own relatives. Almost all of them took an unsympathetic attitude toward my views. They were proud of the many churches in town, and most of them felt that there was no need for any other cultural meeting places. In general, they regarded theater, art, literature, and so forth, as something totally irrelevant to them. Not so that everyone considered these phenomena to be directly harmful or invented by the devil—although even such extreme attitudes were represented—but all agreed with the view that they were completely unnecessary, since there was already a rich, blooming, all-around church life in town.

In this town, in other words, there were sixteen different denominations that professed sixteen divergent interpretations of the Christian doctrine in sixteen different churches. I had long and engrossing discussions with Lutherans, Catholics, Presbyterians, Christian Scientists, Methodists, and other believers. There were not many of them who had any time for so-called worldly culture. And it was easy to see that their churches combated all manifestations of cultural life that did not occur within those churches' own walls.

There are areas in Minnesota, Wisconsin, and Michigan where the churches reign supreme and have such a hold on the inhabitants that one has a feeling of being back in the parishes of Småland a hundred years ago. Hardly any development toward a more all-around, differentiated culture is to be seen. Typical of this narrow spiritual outlook is the position taken by some people toward "worldly books." A middle-aged Swedish-born woman in Escanaba, Michigan, a prominent member of the Lutheran congregation, was seized with great horror when she learned that this author's main activity in life had been the writing of novels. Why, just *to read* novels was a sinful activity— how much more serious was the sin committed by the person who wrote them! And this kindly and considerate lady appealed to me urgently: if I wanted to save my soul from eternal damnation, then I ought to change professions at once. Another Swedish-American lady, also a member of the Lutheran church, happened to see the title of the English translation of one of my novels, *The Earth is Ours!*, and she became very upset. A person

as old as I ought to know, after all, that the earth belonged to
God and not to us humans. Here I had made a statement that
to her involved the most serious blasphemy.

The different church groups, however, fight very energetically
even among themselves. The lack of tolerance for people with
different opinions and different beliefs is as noticeable among
the clergy as among the individual congregation members. In a
small Lutheran church in a Swedish settlement area of Minnesota
I heard my first sermon in America, and it left me feeling de-
pressed. At the beginning, to be sure, the minister in the pulpit
quoted some words from the Scriptures about the commandment
to love our neighbor, but the continuation of his sermon was of
the sort that thoroughly conflicted with the introductory quotation from the Bible. He gave vent in fact to a completely hard-
ened intolerance, where it concerned those of his fellow humans
who belonged to a church other than his own. He denounced
the Catholics and denied that they had any right to call themselves Christians. He made insinuations that all who believed
in Catholicism were following a path leading to eternal damnation. The greater part of his sermon consisted of warnings
against the delusions in religion that all other churches outside
his own represented. Certainly the minister called upon us to
love our neighbor, but if we were to follow the full implications
of his preaching we could consider as our neighbor only those
people who were members of an Evangelical Lutheran congregation.

In other churches since then I have heard other ministers
whose sermons were characterized by the same spirit of intolerance. Now I hasten to add, however, that this is not a question
of a phenomenon that especially characterizes the Swedish
churches in America. The Swedes are by no means in the lead
when it comes to setting a bad example concerning intolerance—
just the opposite: they probably show somewhat greater tolerance in their religious practices than other ethnic groups. If anything, it is the Catholic Church that displays the greatest fanaticism

and implacability; with its twenty-three million members it also represents a tremendous power in the United States.

Now the religious organizations are also a power in this world, and they look after their economic interests carefully and skillfully. Every congregation is also entirely dependent on the generosity of its members for its existence.[7] In the town with the many churches mentioned above, I saw evidence of what great demands can be placed on this generosity. An elderly Swedish lady of modest economic means, who had belonged to the First Lutheran Church in town for nearly fifty years, showed me a letter that she had just received from the church board. In this letter she was reproached in harsh terms because she had made insufficient contributions to her church during the previous year. The letter concluded with an ultimatum: if in the future she was not prepared to make larger monetary contributions to the congregation, then she would be expelled from its fellowship.

The woman considered herself, however, to have made as large an offering to the church as was within her power. Making a person's membership in a church dependent on that person's greater or lesser degree of economic support is, in any case, a procedure that cannot be reconciled with the teachings of Christ. Besides, the congregation in question here was especially well-off, in a material sense, and drew upon a sound economic base. It seems to me, in other words, that it could have placed fewer demands on the generosity of its less well-to-do members.

Spiritual life requires a certain material base for its development, but nowadays this requirement seems to have been met in the Swedish areas of North America. They are rich districts, most of these areas settled by our fellow countrymen, much richer than many parts of Sweden, where the church is of a completely different nature, however. The members of these congregations do not seem, in general, to lack the material resources that are required for the acquisition of education and culture. But the development of the church is not just dependent on the level of education that the *members* of a congregation have been able to acquire, but also—and above all—on the qualifications found in the *leader* of the congregation. It is clearly the clergymen who, above all others, leave their mark on a church; it is the ministers who shape its course.

Now it is obvious that the clergy in the free churches of America do not enjoy the same independent position as the ministers in the Swedish State Church. The pastor of a Swedish parish is a government official and for all practical purposes cannot be dismissed, while the free churches in America, to an unlimited degree, can remove and appoint their clergymen. It follows from this that these latter are forced, to a far greater degree than are their Swedish colleagues, to pay attention to irrelevancies—for example, to powerful members of the church fellowship—a situation that many times surely has been a hindrance to the ministers in the fulfillment of their duties.

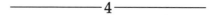

— 4 —

In the year 1880, three of my mother's brothers came to the wilds of Iron County in northern Michigan, three farmer's sons, the oldest twenty-three, the youngest eighteen years old, who had left a farmstead in Småland, subdivided among sixteen families, where the number of children was altogether too great. They had traveled through the woods by foot for 150 miles until they found the place where the little town of Iron River is now located. Here they settled in order to build new homes. My oldest uncle took out a homestead and tried his luck as a farmer; his younger brothers looked for work in the iron ore mines. The former was a deeply religious man, and he was one of the organizers of the first Swedish church in those parts. To commemorate the fact that he was one of the founders of the church, my uncle's name was engraved in his honor on one of its windows. For obvious reasons I was especially interested in visiting this church, and together with the church-builder's daughter—my cousin—I attended the worship service at the First Lutheran Church in Iron River, Michigan, one Sunday.

The Pioneers' Church

The church was filled to the last seat, and after the end of the sermon a man appeared out of the assembled congregation. He walked forward and stood before the altar. The man introduced himself as the representative of a radio shop and offered for sale to the congregation a loudspeaker system that would serve as an amplifier for the church bells. That was only the second time I had ever been in a church in America, and I expected an usher to come up and lead away anyone who disturbed the worship service with a commercial matter. But he was allowed to continue his speech; no one interrupted him. For ten minutes this agent from the radio shop stood before the altar and described his merchandise. He expounded on its low price and on all its other advantages, and in addition to that he pointed out in passing the inferiority of a couple of his competitors' products. And the congregation remained sitting and listened very politely, just as politely as to the preacher's sermon shortly before.

My cousin was very surprised when I later reacted against this odd feature of the worship service, which I did not consider to be best for the devotional spirit in the church. To her the incident was completely commonplace, and she had never for a moment thought about the fact that someone might find it offensive. But to me the episode had illustrated the pioneer character of the church. I had come to see how customs were still being preserved from the time when all the congregation members in town were immigrants and pioneers who did their business in the manner that they found most practical and who discussed all their business in connection with their attendance at church. This practice had no connection with the honesty of their worship or with the seriousness of their religious practices.

Of my uncle—whose name is preserved on the window of the church—it was said that his pew in the temple was not left empty on a Sunday for a period of nearly fifty years. And most of my relatives in the town were still among the regular Sunday churchgoers. It has been said that one cannot rightly understand an American's mentality if one has not delved into his relationship with religion, and to both my relatives and other people I

87

posed the question: Why do you go to church? In most cases I was met with a surprised look that made it clear to me that this was a question that I ought never to have asked, since the answer was obvious: Every decent, upstanding Christian goes to church on Sundays. However, here I believe that only one answer can be given that is satisfactory: I go to church because I feel a need for spiritual edification; I seek communion with my God and Creator. And these reasons were given in a good many cases. But most of the answers ran like this: A Christian just naturally goes to church. To me this was basically an evasive answer that is founded in religious routine and conventionality. There is nothing that tells me that a person is a Christian just because he belongs to a church.

A few times I also got an answer that without a doubt was honest and sincere: I go to church because everyone else I know does so. If I did not do so, I would be in for trouble with my friends and relatives. There were even a few who made this revealing statement: If I didn't go to church on Sundays, then my social standing would suffer and with that my business, too.

In the culturally backward environment that is in question here—the rural areas and small towns of the Midwest and Upper Midwest—a person is not fully respectable, in other words, if he does not belong to a church and attend this church of his on Sundays. Here it is convenient to use religion as a means of gaining advantages in this world: money, power, social status. And examples were presented to me of ambitious citizens, doctors, lawyers, businessmen, and so forth, who were aware of the opportunities that the church can open up for them in their careers. When they open a practice or business in a new town, they immediately find out which church has the largest number of members and consequently the greatest influence, the Lutheran, the Catholic, the Presbyterian, the Methodist, and so forth. And within a short time the biggest and most powerful congregation receives yet another member.

I once heard two ladies, Swedish Americans, discussing a third lady whose respectability had for some reason been questioned.

The Pioneers' Church

In that connection one of the ladies remarked: "I can vouch for her. *She belongs to our church.*" With that, the discussion of the absent lady was concluded at once.

I would like to emphasize once again that these observations on church life in America, which I have here related, refer to a specific, restricted environment and therefore do not lay claim to any general validity. The immigrants and the church—this is a broad subject that I have been able to touch on only very lightly here; it is also an extremely complicated problem, perhaps the greatest and most complicated one that an observer from Sweden meets when, in America, he attempts to delve into the mentalities of the Swedes and Swedish descendants. Here a visitor from Sweden is often left puzzled and unable to understand. One fact ought to be pointed out and emphasized, however: with respect to the church and religion, developments within the separate branches of our national group have proceeded along completely different lines since their separation took place.[8]

CHAPTER 6

What Do Swedes in Sweden and America Know About Each Other?

The separation of the Swedish people into two groups that live in their own parts of the world and are separated by an ocean is a curious example of the division of a nation. We share this fate, however, with several other emigrant nations, for example, Norway and Ireland.

What do they know about each other, these two branches that have grown from the same family tree? First we might ask ourselves: What do we Swedes at home know about the lives of our relatives in their new homeland? I have always had the feeling that our knowledge of them has been incomplete; I did not understand how little we actually know about them until I went to America.

A representative of the cultural elite in Swedish America expressed to me the opinion that our countrymen in America had been practically forgotten by historians and ethnologists in Sweden. He added: Of course Swedish researchers come over here occasionally, but their mission is not to devote time to our own people; instead they generally are going to investigate the relics of some ethnographically interesting Indian tribe. And it appeared to him—from his viewpoint in America—that it would be easier to obtain government grants in Sweden for studying beetles in Madagascar than for scholarly research on some area of Swedish America.

This statement was made by a man who knew what he was talking about—one of the foremost authorities on Swedish America in our time—and it most likely would be difficult to refute it. Swedish historians in particular have shown little interest in that branch of our nation that emigrated to a new part of the world. One example among many that illustrates this: Andrew Peterson's remarkable journal, which for fifty years has been available at a public library in one of the foremost Swedish cities in America, has during this whole time remained completely unknown to researchers on Swedish history.[1]

Without a doubt the Swedish Americans were given attention at an earlier time, in a rather casual manner, by influential cultural groups in Sweden. It is now admitted, even in those circles where I heard the above statement about the lack of opportunity to study Swedishness in America, that the Swedes' interest in their relatives in the United States has been growing steadily during the past decade, both among government authorities and private citizens. A strong contributing factor is the development of communications systems. The ocean has gotten considerably narrower. From a city in the Midwest a letter reaches Stockholm by airmail in three days. The opportunities for contact—and for a steady, ongoing contact—between Sweden and Swedish America by means of correspondence have expanded tremendously and are certain to increase even more. Personal contact still poses insurmountable difficulties for most people; air travel can be utilized by only a few. But the rapid postal service that is in effect nowadays, thanks to airmail, is of that much greater help to Swedes on both sides of the Atlantic.

The contact that has been maintained across the Atlantic by means of the Swedish newspapers in America has been of great importance. In earlier times at least, Swedish Americans often paid for subscriptions to their Swedish-language newspapers for the relatives they had in Sweden. In some cases these "America newspapers" came to Swedish homes where they comprised the only reading material. The first newspapers I read in my life were *Nordstjernan* and *Svenska Amerikanaren*.[2] I cannot remember that I gained any knowledge from them about the lives of the Swedes in America; at that age I lacked interest in the subject. I derived the greatest benefit from the exciting novels in the serialized story section, written by August Blanche, Marie Sophie Schwartz, Emilie Flygare-Carlén, Edel Lindblom, and others.[3] Other boys read local Swedish newspapers with the same serials; in both cases the intellectual benefits were the same. In the "America newspapers" older and more mature people, however, could learn a great deal of value about the country where their relatives lived. These Swedish-American newspapers still find their way to Sweden; *Svenska Amerikanaren Tribunen* in Chicago, for example, sends four thousand copies of each edition to the homeland.

Reading material in Sweden about our countrymen who emigrated to North America is very meager. Especially in the realm of fiction, this one-fourth of our nation has been left completely in the background. What can be the reason for this? The forty thousand Swedes who invaded Russia under Karl XII inspired a great national epic, Heidenstam's *Karolinerna* [*The Charles Men*].[4] During a period of sixty years one million Swedes set out across an ocean and invaded the North American continent—with completely peaceful intentions—but during all this time no writer of Heidenstam's stature has been tempted to depict the undertaking. The trek to the New World by these thousands upon thousands of people left Swedish authors remarkably unmoved, even though it could be looked upon as a greater national catastrophe than the downfall of Sweden as a great power. Now emigration from nineteenth-century Sweden was an irritating phenomenon for the ruling class, a form of reaction against the existing conditions in the country, a symptom of the division of the nation. It was an open and painful wound in the body of the nation that people preferred to avoid touching on. And the historical perspective on emigration could not be established at that time. In addition to this was the fact that it was still to be a few decades before farmers, crofters, industrial and agricultural workers, the classes of people from which the emigrants were mainly recruited, made their appearance in literature in earnest. Perhaps many literate Swedes asked themselves the question: What is going to become of our people in America; what is the destiny they have before them? But the North American continent was still so far away that no one looked for the answer to the question at the scene of events and it was only at the scene that it could be found.

Not until more recent times have native Swedes undertaken studies on the Swedes in America; foremost among the scholarly works that have been published are Professor Helge Nelson's findings on the subject.[5] Unfortunately, his descriptions of the Swedish settlement areas do not circulate outside of professional circles. And there are other books about our emigrants that ought to be better known by the Swedish public. I am thinking, for example, of Gustaf Unonius' remarkable work *A Pioneer in Northwest America 1841–1858,* which I have mentioned before. After his return to Sweden, Unonius published this account of his pioneer life in two large volumes in the years 1861–62. It is a story written by a man who was there himself, and it gives us a wealth of facts that add up to a genuine picture of the times. Unonius has an objective, for the most part sharply focused style; every now and then he tries to fly higher than his wings will bear him and gets lost in outpourings of emotion, but through most of his pages he keeps his feet firmly on the ground. His descriptions of the first pioneers' surroundings in the forests of the state of Wisconsin in the 1840s are completely realistic. Here there is no sickly sweet romanticism of the type found in the great flood of American pioneer novels. At times Unonius can achieve truly epic flight. In the following expressive, vivid sentences he describes, for example, how spring—after a winter of bitter cold when hunger darkened the door of the Swedes' log-timbered house at Pine Lake—finally bursts in upon the settlement, long and eagerly awaited:

"But springtime was bringing forth a wealth outdoors which, even though it did not banish our poverty, at least made it less severely felt. Grass and flowers supplied the cattle with abundant food; once more the forest was swarming with doves and flocks of ducks were swimming on Pine Lake. The *Ellida* was launched on new fishing ventures; a fresh cow gave us plenty of milk; the chickens laid their eggs in bushes and hollows, and the eggs were sold in Milwaukee or exchanged for other goods. Both men and beasts began to revive and to labor with renewed energy."

There is no danger of Unonius' book being taken up by Hollywood. But an association in Swedish America has recently taken the initiative to translate the work into English, one sign among many of the growing interest in the history of the pioneers.[6] The Swedish people have started to become conscious of the fact that they have a history of their own in North America.

Several writers of fiction in Sweden have published depictions of Swedish emigrant life; names such as Fredrika Bremer, Henning Berger, Gustaf Hellström, and Hilma Angered-Strandberg are the first that come to mind.[7] In his first book, a collection of short stories from 1901 *Där ute* [Out there], Henning Berger has created some of the most splendid things we have in this field of study. The author lived in the United States for seven years and managed to acquire a thorough knowledge of the country. In his writings the problems of the immigrants have the genuineness and believability of someone who experienced them himself. Berger's ability to empathize with people whose psyches were destroyed is especially noteworthy. In his short stories the lives of the immigrants are mainly dark and dismal and monotonous: most of his characters are tormented by a homesickness for Sweden that they have no possibility of assuaging. The struggle for survival is hard and bitter, and only the ruthless and unscrupulous are successful. These images are doubtless one-sided and take into account only one aspect of reality; the setting is Chicago in the 1890s, which, everything considered, must have been a frightening city. Above all it was not at that time a suitable place of residence for poets and dreamers; for someone like Berger with an artist's temperament it seemed most nearly like a substation of hell. Other European authors who lived as immigrants in America for longer or shorter periods of time have reacted in similar ways; Knut Hamsun is a familiar example.[8]

Now there is also a Swedish-American literature; by this we mean that literature that has been created by Swedes in America and that has been published in the Swedish language in America. There is even an association of Swedish writers that is active in the United States. This society of writers seems to keep a low profile, however; I never see it mentioned in the Swedish-American press, which is why I assume that it only appears before the general public on exceptional occasions. But Swedish-American literature is of considerable scope. Recently I saw a summary in which no fewer than seventy-some names were listed.[9] This entire literature is, of course, practically unknown to the general public in the old country. My reading in the fictional output of the Swedish Americans is still altogether too scant for me to dare to pronounce any judgment on its quality; it does not appear, however, that any really significant works of literature in Swedish have seen the light of day in America. (A giant in the world of poetry like Carl Sandburg, a Swede of the second-generation, writes in English and belongs, of course, to American literature.)[10] Experts in America assured me, however, that there had been many books published in Swedish that would be worth bringing to the attention of the Swedish public at home: they could serve a purpose, owing to the fact that they would increase our knowledge of the everyday life and customs of our relatives on the North American continent.[11]

We in Sweden need expanded and in-depth information about Swedish America. About this there can hardly be any difference of opinion. And from this viewpoint, no Swedish cultural phenomena, literary or otherwise, ought to be regarded beforehand as irrelevant or insignificant.[12]

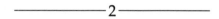

— 2 —

Now we come to the other side of this problem of who-knows-what, namely the question: What do our relatives in America know about us in Sweden?

When a native Swedish visitor in the United States meets his countrymen or their descendants, he has to undergo an exhaustive question-and-answer session on the subject of Sweden. The questions that are aimed at him are extremely varied, but up to 75 percent of them concern that which is understood in the catechism as our daily bread: how we earn our living and get the necessities of life, food and drink, clothes, house and home. They want to know if we are starving or freezing, which essentials are rationed, how things stand in regard to wages and earnings, how the "times" are treating us. And the people doing the asking show by the nature of their questions just how far-reaching a knowledge of Sweden they already possess.

During my stay in the Swedish settlements in six different states, I ran into several hundred people of Swedish descent, from the first to the fourth generation of immigrants. Their knowledge of the land of their forefathers can be summarized in the following manner:

In every town or community where there is Swedish settlement one can meet a few people who keep themselves well informed of developments in the old country and who know the essential facts about us and our daily life. One can also meet people here and there who for totally idealistic reasons are working to preserve Swedish culture and the Swedish language and who in their unselfish efforts do not shrink from sacrificing both time and money. But this applies to a small, select circle of Swedes. The vast majority of those who are descended from Sweden through one or several generations possess scant knowledge about the mother country as it is nowadays. They know about the members of the Swedish royal family and gladly talk about those of our princes who have visited America. They are, of course, well informed about our international film and sports celebrities, and on the whole about those people from back home whose names appear in the American newspapers.

But it would be easy to count up at least a hundred-some Swedes who are household names in present-day Sweden, politicians, scholars, writers, artists, and so on, whom they have never ever heard of. In a large gathering of Swedes in Escanaba, Michigan, I happened to mention Albert Engström[13]—just as someone might mention the name of a person who he assumes is widely known. It turned out that none of those present had heard of him; they were all unaware of who Albert Engström was.

About our intellectual life, our political life, our modern social institutions and popular movements, our social security legislation and our social welfare institutions—about all of this our kinsmen in America have scant knowledge. It is of little importance if someone is uncertain about the question whether Södermanland is a town or a parish in Sweden; most native Swedes would not be able to answer an analogous question concerning the geography of North America. But their imperfect knowledge of modern Sweden is regrettable.

In part we have ourselves to blame for this; Swedish publicity efforts in America, for example, are obviously aimed in the wrong direction. I saw some films about Sweden that were shown to our Swedish descendants; in each case they mainly got to see old pipe-smoking Lapp women, women from Dalarna out raking in their local costumes, teams of folk dancers at Skansen,[14] and so forth. The movies were intended above all else to attract American tourists to Sweden, but they did not supply any information worth mentioning about our country as it is today. The viewers must have gotten the impression that Sweden is a culture preserve from times past, a country that is mainly interesting to antiquarians, which lives shut off from modern development. That which aroused the most interest among the audience was some scenes from modern Swedish agriculture in which they were shown tractors and planters; several people told me of their surprise at the fact that Swedish farmers knew how to handle such things! They had obviously been living under the impression that Swedish farmland was still being tilled with wooden plows and wood-spiked harrows.

About Sweden in times past their knowledge is greater, and this applies above all to those who were born within its borders. A good many of the first generation of immigrants have long ago lost contact with the mother country, however. They have the idea that everything here at home must be the way it used to be—that nothing has changed since the day when they stepped aboard the emigrant steamer. They believe that our country has been left untouched by technological developments and are surprised when they learn that automobiles and airplanes are familiar objects even in the old country. An old Swedish American who emigrated in the 1890s and who had not paid a visit to his homeland listened to me with suspicion when I told him that we could also listen to the radio in Sweden. And when I added that we, with our two million radios, were one of the most assiduous radio-listening nations in the whole world, he appeared to be completely convinced that I was sitting there lying.

The people best informed about Sweden are those countrymen in America who read the Swedish-American press regularly.

It has been predicted several times that our Swedish-language newspapers in the United States—due to the continual Americanization of the immigrants—would be deprived of their means of subsistence and completely disappear within a short time. Despite the sentences of death that have been pronounced on this press, it still lives on. Since the year 1850, around fifteen hundred different periodical publications have been published in the Swedish language in North America ("The Swedish American Press Nears Its Century Mark," by Edgar Swenson, in *The American Swedish Monthly*, August 1948). This figure does not bear witness to an insufficient spirit of enterprise among Swed-

ish-American journalists. Of course, the great majority of these
papers have been granted a life no longer than that of a mayfly.
Of those publications in our language that are still being issued
in the United States and Canada, only about a dozen are newspapers nowadays in the true sense of the word, and as a rule
they are published as weeklies. The oldest Swedish newspaper
in America is *Nordstjernan* in New York, which is publishing its
seventy-eighth volume but which seems younger in spirit than
perhaps any of its counterparts. The newspaper with the widest
circulation is *Svenska Amerikanaren Tribunen* in Chicago, which
has a circulation of sixty thousand copies. Unfortunately, its
editing is extremely pedestrian; it is completely immune to in-
novation and carries on in the same old rut from pioneer days.
In addition, several religious publications are issued in our language in America. An English-language cultural journal, *The
American Swedish Monthly*, should perhaps also be counted as
Swedish since it is published by the Swedish Chamber of Commerce of the United States of America.[15]

Approximately twelve thousand newspapers are published in
the United States today. The Swedish-American press amounts
to a few paltry sheets in this gigantic sea of paper.[16] As I now
renew my acquaintance with these newspapers after a lapse of
forty years, papers that I read so diligently in my childhood, I
meet friends that have changed little through the years. Their
contents are pretty much the same as ever. I recognize the long
columns with small news items from the local districts back home
in Sweden, divided up according to the various provinces; I
recognize the serialized-story section that occupies the same large
and conspicuous place and whose novels as a rule are written
by the same authors from the 1840s: Emilie Flygare-Carlén, Marie
Sophie Schwartz, and others. But modern Swedish literature is
represented above all by Leonard Strömberg, who in religious
circles in Swedish America is considered to be the greatest author
Sweden has ever had.[17] I recognize the local-color stories; even
if the author's name at the end of them is in some cases new,
the contents are the same as before. And I recognize the poems

sent in by readers, touching sentimental stanzas in which home-sickness for Sweden and the Swedish countryside are the motifs that appear most often.

A journalistic tradition from the nineteenth century, which does not give in to changing fashions or trim its sails to fit every shift in the wind, is still alive in most quarters within the Swedish-language press in America. It is a heroic attitude, which in and of itself cannot be faulted. But in those areas where the Swedish-American press is completely bogged down in traditions from the pioneer era, it is threatened with the danger of stagnation.

Now it is close to a miracle that a press as vigorous as this one can still exist in our language outside the mother country. Without idealistic intentions, without dogged, indefatigable effort and great sacrifices from private individuals, it could not have maintained a foothold up to this time. Most of the business assignments that come a person's way in this perverse world must certainly be easier than that of publishing a Swedish newspaper in America. We know of Pastor Hasselquist's hardships with *Hemlandet,* and even if Swedish-American journalists nowadays do not have to struggle with the difficulties of that pioneer editor, the conditions they work under are significantly worse than those of their Swedish colleagues at home. There are still editors of Swedish publications in America who are compelled to set their own type, since Swedish-speaking compositors cannot be found, and with the general decline of the Swedish language the readership keeps dwindling away. The need for daily news is fulfilled by the American press, and only those who are especially interested in happenings in the homeland will stick with a Swedish-language weekly. With all this in mind, a Swedish observer hates the idea of criticizing this press, which works under an entirely different set of circumstances than the press in the mother country, even if he feels that it would have much to gain from a sweeping modernization of content.

Local news items from the Swedish parishes back home are read more than anything else in the Swedish-American newspapers. For an emigrant Swede every happening that occurs in his home parish is an important happening. It takes place in neighborhoods that are well known to him and it concerns people that he knows. A broken leg in Lillmåla, a fiftieth birthday party in Storeby, the dedication of a mission-hall in Mellanhult—these are events that a Swedish American does not overlook in his newspaper. And it supplies important information and helps him to maintain contact with his home area.

But another section in the Swedish-American newspapers appears less indispensable, at least in its present great proportions.

The American press devotes an amount of space to people's purely private doings that is astounding to a European. Anyone who enjoys seeing his name in print, even in the most trivial and meaningless contexts, can have a field day in America. When a person pays a weekend visit to a friend in a neighboring town, he sends a note about the event to the local newspaper, which devotes several long columns in the Monday edition to all of those people who over the weekend have *visitat* each other, as it is called in *svensk-amerikanska*. And an amount of publicity is given to birthday celebrations that invites coldhearted ridicule. Our Swedish newspapers back home are not without sin in this respect and can hardly throw the first stone, but they wait at least until the fortieth anniversary of a person's birth before they start publishing accounts of his birthday. In America they start considerably earlier: a celebrant gets his name in the newspaper as soon as he reaches two years of age. We are given detailed descriptions of the two-year-old's birthday party; the presents for the celebrant are listed, as well as the names of the guests. We get details concerning the color and appearance of the birthday cake with a precise statement of its position on the table, and so on.

Now the Swedish-language newspapers devote proportionately altogether too much space to these personal news items, which to the American press are important news ahead of other items. And it is in this department above all that one might wish for modernization: here a great deal of material of an intimate and familiar nature that I consider to be irrelevant to the general public might with advantage be replaced with copy that informed the readers about modern Sweden.

During the past few years some of the leading Swedish newspapermen in the United States have been invited by our Ministry of Foreign Affairs on study tours of Sweden at the expense of the government, a good idea that has furthered contact between Sweden and Swedish America. The Swedish-American press also receives good assistance nowadays from the American Swedish News Exchange in New York, which was founded in 1921 and which supplies American newspapers with firsthand news releases from Sweden. The name of the institution is somewhat misleading: it has a considerably broader sphere of activity than a normal news service. The American Swedish News Exchange has the job in the United States of distributing factual information about conditions in Sweden and of working chiefly to promote the cultural ties between the countries. It has already done our country an invaluable service in the United States. For more than twenty years its director was Dr. Naboth Hedin, who in that position made a great contribution on behalf of his old homeland. Dr. Hedin, the son of a soldier from Refteled, combines down-home qualities and a knack for practical matters with the theoretical training of a Harvard academician. He retired a couple of years ago from his directorship at the bureau but has a worthy successor in editor Allan Kastrup, formerly of the *Upsala Nya Tidning*, who directs the bureau's affairs very energetically. As far as Sweden is concerned, the American Swedish News Exchange must be considered as an indispensable institution in America; the government funding that is allocated for this undertaking is money well spent, and the allocations should be increased.[18]

Modern Swedish literature is almost unknown in America, and that applies to almost as great a degree in Swedish-American circles as in American ones. Selma Lagerlöf[19] is the only name that is somewhat generally known; only in exceptional cases do people know anything about the authors who made their appearance in literature after her. Heidenstam, Karlfeldt, Lagerkvist, Agnes von Krusenstjerna—these are all unfamiliar names in America.[20] During the last few years, however, Swedish-American newspapers have begun to include literary reviews pertaining to our modern fiction. But as I suggested in the scenes from church life, the Swedish areas of the Midwest and Upper Midwest are totally nonliterary environments; people read newspapers, magazines, and comics, seldom novels, verse, or any sort of fiction.

In this respect, the Swedish Americans are no different, however, from the general populace in the United States. On the average the American people have a higher material standard than ours, but the cultural standards of the great majority of people are lower than in Sweden. As far as I have been able to tell, bookshelves are a more unusual piece of furniture in American homes than in Swedish ones. Even more rarely does one see paintings of artistic value on the walls. A popular cultural organization, such as *Arbetarnas Bildningsförbund* [Workers' Educational Association] here in Sweden, would find virgin fields of endeavor in America.

A rich and highly developed theatrical life flourishes in the largest cities, but the country outside of them seems to be rather badly off as far as the dramatic arts are concerned. Theaters are few; the movie theaters reign supreme. Even a city as large as Minneapolis—with approximately as many inhabitants as Stockholm—is without a permanent theater. In the city of Åbo, twelve thousand Swedes maintain a theater, but no one would come up with the fantastic idea of founding a Swedish theater in, for example, Chicago, where nevertheless there live at least one hundred thousand people who can speak and understand our language. Unfortunately, it is not *the number* of Swedes that is crucial to the maintenance of our culture on foreign soil. A Swede in Åbo and a Swede in Chicago are not comparable individuals.[21]

——————— 3 ———————

There are a good many deficiencies, in other words, in what our relatives on the other side of the Atlantic know about us and our country. But a visitor is delighted by the great hunger for knowledge about things Swedish that they take every opportunity to display. There is no end of questions. Anyone who intends to visit his relatives in the United States will be wise, therefore, to take along information that can be of help during the thorough question-and-answer sessions that he or she will not be able to avoid. A splendid little work on the subject what-to-know-about-Sweden is *Facts About Sweden* (Stockholm: Forum). The book's eighty pages are filled throughout with essential facts that touch on precisely those things that Swedish Americans generally ask about. But of course this little work can only lay the foundation for the knowledge about our country that our inquiring kinsmen are looking for.[22]

In other words, the increased interest in Sweden about our kinsmen in America finds a response in their strong interest in us and our country. The separate branches of our nation are more and more beginning to seek information about each other. They have begun to discover each other—they want to know more about each other.

CHAPTER 7

The Juniper Bush and the Orange Tree

Gothenburg's Maritime Museum has brought together, in a special little exhibit, some authentic materials concerning Swedish emigration to North America: they ought not to be forgotten when the history of this migration one day comes to be written. The museum has even preserved some ship's biscuits that are said once to have been part of the food stores on an emigrant vessel and that in their present petrified state stand a good chance of lasting until Judgment Day before they crumble to pieces.[1] Interesting documents consisting of another material are meanwhile a collection of letters that were written by prospective emigrants to the shipping offices for the ships that transported people to America or to the emigrant ports in England. People usually write requesting information about conditions in the United States, about how "times" are over there. A number of letter writers inquire about the prospects for immigrants in a certain specified state in the Union. And as I went through these letters, it struck me that the state that was mentioned most often was California.

A woman from Ingelstorp wonders "how much a Housekeeper earns per month in California. But is it true that there prevails such a terrible Heat, up to 97 degrees above?" Her hesitancy about the heat is understandable, since the letter writer imagines, naturally enough, that the temperature in California is measured in our own Celsius degrees. A farmer in Ryssby, located in Småland, the land of the juniper bush, wants to know a good deal about the land of the orange trees in America: "Please be kind enough to send to me the information you promised in *Smålands posten* about California, about its agriculture, commerce and cultivation of Oranges, and as you have promised this free of charge I am including no remittance." A third intended emigrant asks only to receive "Maps of California, the largest ones that are in print."

In the year 1930 California showed 41,900 persons born in Sweden. The settlement of our fellow countrymen in that state is of a relatively late date, however; it did not grow to any appreciable proportions before the 1880s and 1890s. Approximately two hundred Swedes were among the hundreds of thousands who took part in the rush to the gold fields in 1848–49. They are responsible for a colorful episode in our emigrant history, but it was only an episode. These panners of gold represented a type of person who in other respects was completely different from our emigrants: they were mainly young, unmarried men, and they did not come to the farthest reaches of the West in order to settle down there for the rest of their lives, but to get rich in the shortest possible time. Swedish newspapers had reported that diamonds the size of hens' eggs and worth 180,000 pounds sterling each could be fished from the Sacramento River with dip nets, and in the year 1849 there had arrived in Gothenburg "samples of California gold" that were found to be of 23 karat. A homespun Swedish song from this era has been preserved, but its author looks on the escapades of the gold panners with a suspicious and wary eye:

> Skåda dessa emigranter,
> som med bländverk i sin håg,
> ifrån jordens alla kanter
> samla sig båd hög och låg

att på Californiens stränder
skörda guld med båda händer.
[Look at these emigrants,
who with their minds deluded,
from all corners of the earth
gather together, both great and small,
in order, on California's shores,
to scoop up gold with both hands.]

It is also reported that only a few of our countrymen got any of the gold. It is right around sixty-five hundred miles between Sweden and the Sacramento Valley; it was a long haul out there and back for those who came home with empty hands.

And it was during these years that such terrible things were taking place under California's mellow sun: the countryside was, to quote a contemporary writer, "a battleground for wild and unbridled passions." Murder and manslaughter took place without the culprits' undergoing any punishment, and stories are told of gaming houses where "on a single card 100,000 *riksdaler* were lost." But it was a lovely and overwhelmingly fertile land, which made a powerful impression on the newcomers. An anonymous Swedish gold panner, for example, writes the following to a newspaper back home: "In this land of California, we have everything in the greatest Abundance and even more. We are short of only one thing here, and that is Women."[2]

And documentary accounts, which I have studied, make it clear that the shortage of women was a very serious problem that contributed to the rise of disorder and acts of violence. After a short period of activity within these gold districts, which had an almost exclusively male population, a prostitute could clear out in a position of economic independence. In a newspaper item from the year 1849 the problem appears in a concrete light:

"Under the leadership and management of Mrs. Farnham the vessel *Angelique* has sailed from New York before midsummer of 1849 bound for California with a cargo of beautiful girls, among them even a few coloreds, in order to relieve the shortage of women existing there."

That was California a hundred years ago. The centennial commemoration of the great gold rush is now being celebrated with a new, even greater migration to the largest of the Pacific Coast states. Now people are coming mostly from the other states of the Union. It is estimated that nearly a thousand people a day move into California. The population is made up for the most part of immigrants of the first generation; a person seldom meets anyone who was born within the borders of the state.[3] Here new homes are being put up in overwhelming numbers; here people are building and raising crops; here human life is somehow new and young as if it had just now begun—here there is still pioneer country and a pioneering spirit. Quite frankly I believe that a person could describe California as the last pioneer state in the United States of America.

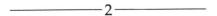

2

When inhabitants of California give expression to their pride in being inhabitants there, they say: it was a great stroke of luck for the future of the United States that Columbus came ashore on the east coast of North America and that the country was settled, as a result of this, from the east to the west; if the first settlers had landed instead on the west coast, in California, no one would have left that country and the rest of the continent would have remained uninhabited.

Personally I consider the regional patriotism of the Californians to be well founded. I was captivated by the state myself. I went there in order to stay a few months, and I remained for a year.[4]

I shall long remember my first sight of the California countryside. It was early one October morning when I looked out through the window of my compartment on the Exposition Flyer; the train was passing through a paradise. We traveled through a deep valley that was a single continuous verdant expanse of fruit trees. The area was so large that a person could not call it an orchard. I have to use the word *forest:* I looked out over a forest of luxuriantly green fruit trees. And where glades opened in this forest, the ground lay covered by a multitude of flowers: bright, slender flowers that shone like burning altar candles. Around the valley that enclosed this paradise on earth, towered the mountains like giant blue waves, halted and held in suspension on their path across the ocean. And above the singularly fresh greenery of this landscape, the sun beamed down from a sky that seemed fresher and more azure than any other heaven I have seen arching over our earth.

In this state lives the largest group of my American relatives, and now I was coming here in order to make the acquaintance of these relations. Previously I had not met any of them, and with only a couple had I been in contact by letter. To me they were in every way the unknown relatives.

Now my meeting with my unknown relatives in California might also—and in the best way of all perhaps—be portrayed in dramatic form. I would begin my play like this:

The Juniper Bush and The Orange Tree

A Play in One Act

CHARACTERS: 28 American citizens and 1 Swede.
SETTING: The lawn of a home in the city of San Leandro, outside of San Francisco, California.
TIME: An evening in the month of October, 1948. The action takes place during a party.

The lone Swede performing on the stage was of course the author himself, a foreigner and guest at the party. The other people, the twenty-eight Americans, were all relatives of his. The owner of the backyard stage was my mother's sister; she had arranged this party so that the newly arrived guest from Sweden might get to meet the other twenty-seven relatives.

Have any of you, you who read this, ever had the experience of being brought together, on one and the same evening and in the same place, with twenty-seven relatives whom you are meeting for the first time in your life? Have you ever entered into a whole little convention consisting of persons who are completely unknown and totally unfamiliar to you, all of whom count themselves as your relatives, more or less? Have you had the experience of being introduced twenty-seven times in a row in the same evening to a completely unfamiliar person who says: I am your cousin, I am your cousin's wife, or I am your cousin's son, and so on, and so on? By the time we got to the twelfth person, I thought it was beginning to get monotonous: this certainly seemed repetitious. Introduction—hug—kiss-on-the-cheek: that is the ceremony when relatives meet in California, where the people are more Mediterranean in temperament than in the rest of the United States. Thus: twenty-seven hugs in succession by unfamiliar people, twenty-seven kisses on the cheek by the same people. In a stage play this scene that was set in a yard in San Leandro, California, when I met my American relatives, would have been incredibly tedious, but in real life anything can happen once: no one has the ability to strike out lines from the manuscript of Our Lord, which we call Life.

And the scene was a challenge to me in several respects. I had a feeling that I had joined as a participant in an especially uneven game. The guests at this garden party were divided into two groups: my relatives constituted one of these groups; I alone made up the other. I had come to California in order to meet them; they had come to this party to meet me. But my relatives met only *one* unfamiliar person while I was meeting twenty-seven *strangers*—I was supposed to get acquainted with and concentrate my attentions on twenty-seven unfamiliar people. In this way I was tremendously handicapped. The others were only supposed to get to know me, but I was supposed to get to know all of them. Twenty-seven against one—we played an uneven game on that field.

110

Juniper Bush and Orange Tree

But it was a beautiful field, that lawn in San Leandro, on the mild and warm October evening that resembled an evening in the beginning of August back home in Sweden. We sat there under orange, peach, and apricot trees and drank light California wine, and our meeting place was luxuriantly enclosed by a hedge of grapevines on which the clusters of ripening black grapes glistened in the light.

My relatives were eager to know about me and I about them. But their appetite for knowledge was so infinitely more easy to satisfy than mine: they only had to figure out one person; I had to figure out twenty-seven.

I had made up my mind, however, that I was going to satisfy my curiosity in one respect at least: I was going to determine the real *nationality* of my relatives. Only one of those present—the hostess, my aunt—was born in Sweden. All of the others were born in America, and the very youngest ones were Swedish descendants of the fourth generation. But how much Swedish blood did they now have left in them and with which nations had they mingled their blood? That was the question I wanted to ask those present.

And I asked it, as I see it, in an effective—American!—manner. At one time when I was a journalist I learned a few things that I have since made use of.[5] And now I quite simply played the role of an interviewer: I took a pencil and paper and went from relative to relative and asked each and every one the same question: Aside from the fact that you are an American—*what nation do you come from?*

This method brought quick results, and I read the results out loud to those gathered there: the group of relatives that was present represented eleven European nations. There were eight Swedes, two Norwegians, two Finns, three Scots, two Irish, two Englishmen, one German, one Frenchman, one American, one Swiss, and one Spaniard. Besides that, I was related to four persons whose nationality appeared so complicated that I did not want to take on the responsibility of deciding it. How would you describe a person, for example, whose father was half-German and half-Mexican and whose mother was half-Swedish and half-Scottish? Or how would you denote the country of origin for the young man—the son of one of my cousins—who answered my question like this: "My father had a Swedish mother and a Spanish father; my mother was born to a mother who was half-Irish and half-Norwegian and to a father who was half-German and half-American. Now what would you call me?"

That gathering at my aunt's house in San Leandro was a family reunion. But I assume that it is more the exception than the rule that representatives of eleven different nations show up at family reunions.

And the hostess for the evening also had a feeling of the unique character of the gathering. She said: "This is no ordinary garden party, you see; this is a meeting of the United Nations."

That was the most fitting remark of the evening.

Now people of full Swedish nationality were by no means in the majority at this family reunion, even though they had more representatives than any other nation. And I began to lose myself in thought and meditate about the infusion of Smålandish peasant blood that flowed through the veins of most of those present. I thought about Småland's contribution to this microcosm of Europe that had migrated to American soil and that now lived and prospered under the generous California sun.

Småland and California—what areas on earth could be more different from each other? What a diverse pair: Småland, my poor, meager home area, the stone-land of Sweden, and rich, fertile California, the pride and joy of America! In the one landscape rough pastures with cranberry bogs and tufts of cowberries; in the other sun-bathed mountain slopes with palm trees and grapes. The juniper bush on the barren heath; the orange tree in sweet, flowery Eden. Here are to be seen truly dramatic opposites—such stuff as plays are made of.

A twelve-year-old girl in the group, belonging to the fourth generation, suddenly asked me a question: "Is Sweden in Europe or in Africa?" (By way of explanation it should be noted that geography instruction in American schools is rather cursory as far as countries located outside the American continent are concerned.) The girl who asked me this question was the great-great grandchild of a farmer from Småland.

These unfamiliar people, who were my relatives, had from the beginning taken it for granted that I would make a speech at the reunion, and so now they sat there and waited for me to start in on the talk. I had been wracking my brain for a long while about what I was going to say to them, but when the girl brought up her geographical question about the old country it hit me all of a sudden: I decided to talk about farm people in Småland, about a man and a woman who had been dead for a long time, about a man who for three-quarters of a century had lain in his grave in the cemetery of the parish where he was born. It became clear to me at once that a Swedish farm couple from the middle of the last century were very important people there that evening, in that American gathering, in that glorious California countryside.

And so I began to tell about the farmer Aron Petters Son—as he wrote his name[6]—from Algutsboda parish in Kronoberg County, my mother's father. It was he who was the great-great grandfather of the schoolgirl who had just wondered if Sweden was in Europe or in Africa.[7]

Aron Petters Son was born in the year 1830. In the year 1856 he entered into marriage with Johanna Johans Dotter from Duvemåla in the same parish and took over the family farm Moshultamåla, a crown farmstead already subdivided among sixteen of his family members. His plot consisted of seven acres of rocky fields and supported five cows and one horse. The farmhouse, where he also was born, contained two rooms and a kitchen; it was torn down about twenty years ago. During his marriage to Johanna Johans Dotter seven children were born, five sons and two daughters.

Aron Petters Son could read reasonably well, but his writing ability was limited to his being able to print his name. His wife could read but not write.

Aron Petters Son passed away on the first of May, 1875, only forty-five years old. At his death the oldest child was seventeen years old, the youngest two. According to the records from his property settlement, which I have in my possession, the total assets of the dead man came to 3,102 *kronor* and 50 *öre* and the debts to 2,577 *kronor* and 41 *öre*. Since half of the remaining sum in his estate fell to his widow, the other half was divided up and distributed to the seven children as their inheritance, with 37 *kronor* and 53 *öre* going to each of them.[8]

Six of the seven children, all the sons and one of the daughters, emigrated to North America during the 1870s and 1880s. The daughter who stayed at home later became my mother.

When the children who were fit to work left home, the widow was forced to sell the family farm. My parents bought it back in 1907. Grandmother went into retirement and lived alone in one of the two rooms in the farmhouse. She survived Grandfather by thirty-seven years and died in 1912, eighty years old. Four of the children who emigrated she never saw again. She could not write letters herself to her children in America, or read the letters from them either.[9]

Five of the children of Aron Petters Son and his wife got married in America and had thirty-four children of their own altogether. These grandchildren were my cousins, in other words. During my several months' stay in America, I had met most of them, but far from all. And I had no way of telling the number of children in the third generation. Besides, there was already a fourth generation that had now reached school age and that liked to ask questions about Sweden.

I figured out that approximately one hundred or so descendants of Aron Petters Son were living within the borders of the United States at the time. One son and one daughter of his settled in this state, California, where their children, grandchildren, and great-grandchildren now made their homes. And it was that branch of the family that I had the privilege of meeting that evening at this pleasant and memorable party. It turned out, in this connection, that through intermarriage in America with people of ten other nationalities they nowadays made up a microcosm of Europe, of the Old World.

I told those present much more than this about their family roots in the Old World, on a little farm in Småland, a piece of property subdivided among sixteen farmers, but it is of no interest in this context.

From that family reunion and garden party only this remains to be added, that two people who were not present, who departed this world many years ago, were the most important and most noteworthy guests in that beautiful and flowering lawn in the city of San Leandro, California: the farmer Aron Petters Son from Moshultamåla and his wife Johanna Johans Dotter. These two had the starring roles in my play: two dead people in invisible guise were the main characters on stage.

Aron Petters Son and his wife were the roots and the cause of this meeting between twenty-eight American citizens and one Swede, of this assembly of the United Nations, of this meeting between Småland and California—between the juniper bush and the orange tree.

CHAPTER 8

How the Swedes Become Americans

The first emigrants to North America departed this world more than half a century ago; practically all of their children have passed away; and their grandchildren have passed middle age. It is their great-grandchildren—the fourth generation—who are now entering the best and most productive years of their lives. And as far as the descendants of the more recent emigrants are concerned, it is Swedish descendants of the second and third generations who are in the prime of life in America today.

These citizens of Swedish descent in the United States are enjoying the fruits of their parents' and forefathers' pioneer achievements, and as a rule they live in comfortable circumstances in the country with the world's highest standard of living. They are Americans and view themselves as totally American. Seldom does a person meet anyone among them who understands Swedish and even more seldom anyone who can speak the language. Our language is spoken almost exclusively nowadays by those who remain alive from the first generation of immigrants, by those who were born in Sweden. The children of Swedish parents speak English. In some families one can hear the parents speak to their children in Swedish while the children answer in English. Children and young people understand their parents' language, but they have difficulty speaking it and they

116

prefer English, which they use in school and in their dealings with everyone outside the home. Swedish is best preserved in out-of-the-way areas of the countryside, among the farmers. In Chisago County in Minnesota I heard, to my surprise, a third-generation farmer speak the same genuine Småland dialect that I remember hearing from my grandmother. He had studied the language in grade school—that Swedish school no longer exists now—and with his parents, who in turn had learned it from their parents, who came from Småland. In this way Swedish country dialects are preserved in America even after they have begun to disappear in Sweden; I believe that the Swedish settlements over there would be a richly rewarding field of activity for dialect specialists from Sweden, however strange that may sound.[1]

Americans of Swedish extraction have only in exceptional cases visited Sweden. Some have inquired into their Swedish origins and are very familiar with them; others are completely unversed in the subject. Whenever I asked any of them about their relatives' home district in Sweden, it might happen that I got this answer: My paternal grandfather was born in a little town that is called Västmanland. Or: My maternal grandmother came from the parish of Värmland in the county of Torsby. Or: My paternal grandfather was born in the parish of Jönköping in the district of Skillingaryd. An elderly lady in Minneapolis asked me if I knew of a place in Sweden that was called Prästgården: it was from this very place that her parents had emigrated at one time.[2] She did not want to believe me when I explained that there is a building in every Swedish country parish that is called Präst-gården and that because of this her parents' birthplace was difficult to locate—she insisted that this was a question of a specific place in Sweden by that name.

The descendants of our emigrants have managed to put a lot of distance between themselves and Sweden; they find themselves further removed from the country than their grandparents, not in terms of distance but in other respects. They are—in contrast to the first Swedish Americans—deeply and irrev-

117

ocably rooted in a new country. At times old-line Swedish Americans feel divided between the old country and the new, and it happens that they are haunted by feelings of homelessness. The old home area still dominates their dreams, and they long to return; as a rule, however, they are quickly cured of their longing after only a short visit to the old country and return to America completely satisfied. But their children and grandchildren are free of this divided heart; in their case there exist no romantic passions for the old home place, called forth by childhood memories. Instead their interest in Sweden is thoroughly matter-of-fact and unsentimental.

The Swedes, in other words, are mixing in with the great masses of people in America and disappearing among them. For Swedish patriots of conservative vintage, this spectacle is perhaps distressing. But it is meaningless to consider this process from a narrow nationalistic viewpoint and equally meaningless to lament it. Not even *Riksföreningen för svenskhetens bevarande i utlandet* [The Swedish Association for the Preservation of Swedishness in Foreign Countries][3] sees it as its duty to try to combat developments in America. This process of assimilation is a matter of course and necessary. It would not in any way be a gain for our fellow countrymen to try to establish a few Swedish culture preserves in America. Sweden must console herself with the fact that Swedish Americans are maintaining important aspects of their ancient cultural heritage—even in their capacity as Americans.

2

The United States of America is a unique creation in the history of the world: representatives from all the nations of the world have joined forces here to found a new nation. Above all, America contains all of Europe within its borders; more than anything else it is Europe, transplanted to new soil.

During his first period of time in the United States, a foreigner can easily get the impression that daily life there is standardized, uniform, and unvaried. But after he has extended his stay for a while and moved around a bit on this vast continent he will make new, surprising discoveries. There is a certain mentality, a certain distinct way of thinking, a certain outlook on life that is the same for the great majority of America's inhabitants. There is something that is called the *American way of life*. But when one gets closer to the people, one begins to wonder if there is any country in the world that contains a wider range of variations in respect to ways of life than these United States. It is a country for individualists. Here there are indeed nuances and differences. Here people of radically different races and nationalities make their homes, and yet to a great extent they have maintained their distinctive character. All of the languages of the world are spoken here; newspapers and books are published here in most of the existing languages; all the world's religions are preached here; all the folk dances of the world are danced here; all the folksongs of the world are sung and all the folk costumes of the world are worn here; every food in the world is eaten and all the beverages of the world are drunk here; all the national customs of the world are observed here. And all of these activities take place among a people who live under a common authority and have a common government.

Here, of course, the reader interjects: But an American represents a certain standardized type of person that is easy to recognize. Then I ask: What is an American?

Since I have traveled around among the people who inhabit North America, I now understand better how homogeneous we Swedish people are. We are *one nation*. But I know of no one expression that covers what the inhabitants of America are. What, for example, do the Scandinavian and German farmers in Minnesota have in common with the Mexican fishermen in California? A farmer in Minnesota of northern European descent is settled, industrious, thrifty, conscientious, sober, religious, and in his entire disposition a puritan. He is generally well-to-do, belongs to the Republican party, is an isolationist, and hates Roosevelt and all recollection of him. A Mexican fisherman is at

119

times not even settled. He can live in concrete culverts and old steam boilers. He is usually poor, lazy, wasteful, slovenly, drunk, never goes to church and professes no other religion than that of carefreeness, even if he is technically speaking a Catholic. He belongs to no political party and never votes for president; he has possibly heard of Roosevelt but knows hardly anything about his political platform and it does not interest him the least bit either.

Both of these people, whose mentalities have here been sketched with a few broad strokes, appear, in other words, to be different in every essential way. And if they met, they would simply not have anything to say to each other, even though they could make themselves understood, each one in his own dialect of English. What unites them is their citizenship in this great republic: they are both Americans. But which one of the two is the typical American?

The example given above is not an extreme case. A person could take the Negroes, the Chinese, the Japanese and point out the wide gap that opens up between colored people and whites in the United States. The concept "American" is a broad concept.

But then we come to the Yankees, the backbone of the American nation, who can trace the history of their settlement in North America several hundred years back: they are the standard-bearing class, the Americans in the narrowest sense of the term. I did not come across many of those who are conventionally regarded as typical Americans—they are not easy to meet up with—and I will therefore refrain from trying to describe them. But it is their way of life and mentality that the younger people in America—and among them our Swedes—have accepted and made their own, to a greater or lesser degree.

It has been argued that Swedes on foreign soil lose their nationality more quickly than other people. It has been said that our race in the United States allows itself to be Americanized more unresistingly than other nations. I dare not decide if this observation is correct, even if there is much that speaks for it.[4]

How Swedes Become Americans

There are, nevertheless, many of our people over there who have successfully asserted their distinctive Swedish character in spite of the fact that they have never seen Sweden. Yet it appears to me as if the Norwegians and the Irish, for example, have succeeded better than our own people in maintaining their distinctive national identities. The Norwegians and the Irish both belong to individualistic nations, cocky people with a strong aversion to following the herd. The fact that these individualists feel at home in America proves that there is a good deal of freedom in this country, a country so badly vilified by champions of freedom who have never visited it.

Before I went over there, I knew that I had nearly a hundred or so relatives in America, a natural result of the fact that the children of two whole families emigrated from Småland in the nineteenth century, in one case leaving behind only a boy, in the other only a girl. Both of these persons who remained at home later became my parents. Thus, with these exceptions, there were two whole families who emigrated. I often pondered the fate of the emigrants in the New World and sought to imagine what these people were like who had come from the same roots as I. I understood, of course, that the new generations of my relatives were no longer primarily Swedes, but Americans. But what I could not picture to myself back home was their widely varying national origins from countries in Europe. I did not count on the fact that my relatives had become so strongly intermixed with other peoples through marriage.

During my time in America, I met around seventy people with whom I could claim family ties, more or less. This group of relatives represents—not counting Sweden—fourteen different European nations.

Thus I was able to observe on the spot how our people had intermixed with other nationalities through marriage and had been transformed into Americans. There is nothing to say about the developments that are taking place here; the Swedes would not be doing themselves any favor by practicing inbreeding. To the extent that I have been able to make observations within my own group of relatives, I think their mixing with other nationalities has shown good results. The cool and sluggish blood of the Swede has been provided with a much-needed dash of high spirits from people of other nationalities, so that Swedish energy, tenacity, and enterprise have been complemented by a versatile intellect and a lively temperament—traits that are generally not characteristic of us Scandinavians.

To what nationalities are the Swedes in America now getting married, besides to other Swedes? With which peoples are they entering into that union that is aimed at the propagation of the species? No far-reaching conclusions may be drawn from those marriages that are entered into within a small group of people who, as is the case here, are defined by a specific common origin. But as far as the male members of my American family are concerned, the Irish people seem to have had the greatest power of attraction: four of my male cousins are married to Irishwomen and two of the female cousins to Irishmen. And at least the former I understand very well: of all the women I have met in America the Irish women are the most charming, to use a trite expression. They are spontaneous, natural, feminine, humorous, and never prudish or affected. They are also regarded as hot-blooded in respect to sex. As far as my cousins' wives are concerned, I would in a couple of cases even like to quote Birger Jarl's words to Bengt Lagman when the former beheld the latter's wife for the first time: "Had my brother left this undone, then I myself would have . . ." I had heard many times before that a strong antagonism was supposed to exist between the Swedes and the Irish in America, but my experiences do not point that way at all. I have also very much liked the male representatives of the Irish people that I have met. They have been original, gifted with imagination, truly kindhearted—in a word: human in the best sense of the word. Ireland in America is truly a positive experience. And the country I would most like to visit now is Ireland in Europe: if the American version of this people is so charming, then what must the original source itself be like . . .!

How Swedes Become Americans

And the children of those Swedish-Irish marriages that I know of do not seem to have anything wrong with them. Maybe from the viewpoint of our Swedish penchant for orderliness, they are somewhat undisciplined and ill-mannered, but they have these bad habits in common with American children in general. In America it is sometimes rather difficult to carry on a conversation with parents in the presence of their children, as it is the children who decide what people are going to talk about; to the great delight of their parents, they constantly interrupt their elders' conversation. And it appeared to me that the spirited Swedish-Irish youngsters, blissfully unrestrained by any discipline, took special pains to provide their parents with this pleasure.

Among my group of relatives in America, the mixture of Swedes and Scots has also resulted in charming individuals, in a couple of cases definite talents: two of my female cousins are married to Scottish men. Now we Smålanders already have a tie to the Scottish people by way of a well-known, common quality: stinginess, the disposition toward economy that borders on greed. It was because of this that I looked ahead with a certain anxiety and apprehension to making the acquaintance of people who had been born out of a Småland-Scottish marriage. It turned out that they were the most carefree and generous and, in respect to economy, the most open-handed people that I have met here in this life of mine. They had absolutely no money, but if they had had any I would have been able to borrow every last cent of it. Without a receipt.

Every now and then I was able to observe how certain external family features of our Swedish descent had been preserved all the way to the third and fourth generations. In marriages with predominantly foreign blood—Irish, German, French, or Spanish—there have been born children who display something easy to recognize: my maternal grandfather's large, unusually strongly defined nose, my maternal grandmother's powerful, unusually well-developed chin. Once I met a woman to whom I am very distantly related but who was so much like my mother in her

123

younger days that I stood there totally dumbfounded when I met her. Such concrete evidence of common roots and a common origin awakens a special feeling of affinity with our relatives in America.

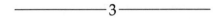

3

The first-generation immigrants are for the most part zealous American patriots; in this respect they surpass those Americans whose families have lived in the New World for several hundred years. Their patriotism can manifest itself in idiotic and ridiculous ways. In Tennessee Williams' play *A Streetcar Named Desire*—known in Sweden by the title *Linje Lusta*—there is a magnificent line that reveals this immigrant mentality; the line is spoken by the full-blooded Pole Stanley:

"If you want to know what I am, I'm 100 percent American, born and raised here in the best country on earth, and I'm damned proud of it! Remember that, and don't call me a Polack again!"[5]

A smugness of this type is found among self-important immigrants, who are not Americans in any sense other than that they have succeeded in taking out their citizenship papers after a five years' stay in the country. The closer an American citizen is to his European origins, the more satisfied he is with America and the more often he joins in with the preachers of vulgar patriotism. The inferiority complex that is expressed here is especially noticeable in Eastern and Southern Europeans who have emigrated from countries with feudal governments; it seems to occur less commonly among people from Northern and Central Europe.

Those Swedish descendants in America who have feelings of inferiority on account of their origins would probably be easy to count. I never met any individual who in any way sought to conceal his Swedish extraction; just the opposite, people often and readily pointed it out with obvious pride. If an American has a Swedish grandmother or grandfather or some even more distant ancestor from our nation, then he does not forget to mention it. Swedish descent appears to be something almost high-class nowadays. Here a marked change has set in: in the past it was not so uncommon that the Swedes were looked down on in America. They came from a poor and backward country that hardly anyone had heard of, they were poorly dressed, and they came with their red-striped satchels that looked a little ridiculous. And their complete ignorance of the English language was a great hindrance to them. Older Swedish Americans told me stories about all the humiliations they had to endure during their first years in the country because they could not answer when they were spoken to. "Roundheads" was one of the nick-names that were given to the Swedish immigrants.[6] There is no use either in hiding the fact that we Swedes are not known as an especially quick-witted people, regardless of whether we have remained in Sweden or emigrated to foreign countries. But our nation has other qualities that are acknowledged and appreciated in America: integrity, honesty, industriousness, an enterprising spirit, a sense of order, energy, technical abilities. It is owing to these qualities that the Swedes have made their contributions in America; with them they have won esteem and respect. Their homeland has also changed completely during the course of the past hundred years; the Sweden of today is a different country from the Sweden of the Four Estates, from which those people who were despised at home emigrated, only to be celebrated as heroes a hundred years later.

As the Swedes have been assimilated into American society, they have changed as a social group. Our relatives now represent a considerably greater number of occupations and professions than they did half a century ago. The large majority of our emigrants came from the laboring classes and in America they sought a livelihood as manual laborers. They became farmers, lumberjacks, railroad workers, miners, craftsmen, factory work-ers. Their children and grandchildren, who have been educated in America, have followed what we in Sweden call the white-cuff professions: they are businessmen, office workers, engi-neers, teachers, and so forth. It is reported that four hundred

Swedish descendants are employed today as professors at American universities. Taken quantitatively, the Swedes are not especially prominent, however, in the intellectual professions; agriculture, the trades, and industry are still the areas in which we most often find them. Our fellow countrymen are especially well known as skillful building contractors and carpenters. An American expert in California explained to me that Swedish contractors in that state had done a "very creditable job."

It is obvious that the Americanization of our fellow countrymen is progressing more quickly now than in the past, which is mainly a result of the fact that the children of Swedish parents are seldom given any school instruction in the Swedish language nowadays. In all the Swedish settlements I visited, the Swedish grade schools had been closed down.[7] In the churches the official language for religious services is generally English. Swedish is still used but is steadily being superseded. On several occasions I heard older Swedish immigrants complain about the fact that they no longer got to hear their mother tongue from the pulpit; it was only with difficulty that they could understand a sermon in pure English; they spoke what we call *svensk- amerikanska*. In the past it might happen that Swedes lived almost their whole lives in America without learning the new language; they stayed within areas of Swedish settlement and associated primarily with their fellow countrymen, and consequently had no need of any language other than their mother tongue. But that time is now past. How well an immigrant in this day and age succeeds in improving his lot in America is to a large extent dependent on his greater or lesser degree of proficiency in English. Swedish is neglected and forgotten for the reason that people no longer have any use for it in the practical world.

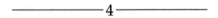

— 4 —

Through the years the United States of America has demonstrated an amazing ability to keep those people who have come to the country from other parts of the world. Here we have one

of the reasons why the United States, in a shorter time than any
other country that appears in world history, has developed into
a world power. The American nation is still only 174 years old.
Neither Rome nor America was built in a day, but America was
built in considerably fewer days than Rome.

People have come to North America to seek new homes for
themselves, but the country has been able to keep even those
who have come on other business. During the War of Independence in the 1770s, England shipped across to America, among
other things, an army of five thousand men consisting of German
mercenaries, who were supposed to aid in humbling the rebel-
lious colonists. When this army was to be shipped out and sent
home to Europe again after the armistice, according to the terms
of the peace treaty, it turned out that it had disappeared, it was
nowhere to be found. The army no longer existed; it had dis-
banded and vanished. Where had the soldiers gone? They had
quite simply deserted, one and all, and settled down as pioneers
in that foreign land!

In his *History of the United States* André Maurois comments on
the event in this way: "So great was this virgin continent's power
of assimilation that it changed into citizens those men who had
come here as enemies."

And it has not been adequately impressed upon the minds of
our people that our relatives in America are citizens of a country
that has the world's oldest democracy. When the United States
laid the groundwork for its constitution in the year 1776, we still
had royal despotism in Sweden—during Gustav III's last years
and during all of Gustav IV Adolf's reign. There were still almost
150 years left until 1918.[8] In comparison with democracy in the
United States, our own democracy dates from yesterday.

A historian of Swedish extraction at the University of Minnesota said to me on one occasion: "Every time a new tyrant
has appeared among you in Europe, we have gotten a portion
of the Old World's best people over here in America: the insurgents, the revolutionaries, the rebels, the freedom fighters.
And they have been of invaluable aid to us Americans: they have

helped us to uphold and develop our traditions of freedom. We truly have a lot to thank Europe's tyrants for!"[9]

And this is nothing other than the unchallengeable testimony of world history; throughout the ages, the Europeans have sought freedom on the American continent after they have lost it in their homelands. They fled from oppression by the church in the 1600s; they fled from the autocratic rule of emperors and kings after the unsuccessful rebellions of 1848; they fled from Hitler in the 1930s; they are fleeing from Stalin today.

More than a million Swedes and their descendants, up to the fourth and fifth generations, have been united with the people of the United States. We can rest assured that our kinsmen have been assimilated by the very people who stand out as the most powerful defenders of human freedom in the world today.

CHAPTER 9

Twenty Years Later

The contents of this book were written during my stay in the United States in the years 1948–50, and the first edition of the book came off the press in 1950. Twenty years have elapsed, in other words, since *The Unknown Swedes* was written. A lot can happen during such a long time, especially in an age like ours, a century of great upheaval. As far as the United States is concerned, the basis for my characterization of that country, which the last sentence of my book ended with in 1950, has been completely shattered by later developments. In 1968, therefore, my work demands a postscript.

A concise summary of the changes during the past twenty years can be expressed in this way: the United States is no longer the country to which rebels and revolutionaries flee. Instead it is precisely this group of people that is leaving the United States today and going into exile in Canada and Europe.

At the moment I write this, it is reported that about twenty thousand soldiers have deserted from the United States Army and gone to Canada. An unknown number of young Americans has run away from the military service in their homeland and fled to Europe; around one hundred of them have sought and received asylum in Sweden. Soldiers no longer desert *to* the North American republic; they run away *from* it. American citizens are looking in other countries for the freedom that they

129

consider themselves to have lost in their native land. The remarkable thing that has happened is that the stream of refugees has been reversed—in the past it went from east to west, but today it goes in the opposite direction. And it consists not only of deserters who do not want to bear arms but also of Americans who on account of general opposition to and protest against developments in their homeland have become emigrants from America.

That which is happening appears to me to be an extremely disturbing symptom of conditions in the United States in the year 1968.

Twenty years ago who could have imagined Americans as refugees in other countries? Even though these Americans are still few in number, their very presence is a sign of an extraordinarily serious development in the United States. Those who are leaving the country, in fact, represent a select group of citizens. To me these Americans are carrying on their country's great traditions of freedom; they are truly faithful to these traditions; they are Americans who do not want to betray the proud message in the Declaration of Independence of the 4th of July, 1776.

The United States is losing rebels, insurgents, freedom fighters, the very type of people who laid the foundation for the American Union. Now that the United States has become the most powerful country in the world, the upholders of this tradition are going into exile.

Has the United States lost the ability, which I pointed to above, of keeping its people? What has happened to the United States? This question is being asked by everybody who, like me, has followed developments during the past few years with profound disappointment.

For an answer that would get to the heart of the matter and its true causes volumes would be required, so great is the subject. And yet it is mainly to be found in a single phrase: *The Vietnam War*.

Twenty Years Later

─────── 2 ───────

First I will go back in time in order to explain how the political situation in the world has changed. Twenty years ago Europe was dominated by the fear of the Soviet Union's expansionist politics. Beginning in 1940 and continuing on to 1948, the Stalin regime had subjugated Estonia, Latvia, Lithuania, East Germany, Poland, Hungary, Rumania, and Bulgaria and established communist dictatorships in each of those eight countries. In February of 1948, Soviet aggression was extended to a ninth country, Czechoslovakia, where power was seized practically overnight by a small minority that was supported by Russian troops. The coup in Czechoslovakia came as a shock to the West and aroused such strong public opinion in Europe's remaining democracies that it might be described as the straw that broke the camel's back. The threat from Eastern Europe was so alarming to the countries of Western Europe that a defense alliance between them was considered necessary. So in Washington on the fourth of April, 1949, there came into being the defense treaty that was named the Atlantic Pact and that had the objective of deterring the Soviet Union from an attack against Western Europe.

Originally joining forces in the Atlantic Pact were Belgium, Canada, Denmark, France, Iceland, Italy, Luxembourg, the Netherlands, Norway, Portugal, Great Britain, and the United States of America. Later West Germany, Greece, and Turkey entered into the alliance. The Atlantic Pact countries came to no fewer than fifteen in number. In the fifth and most important article of the pact—it has fourteen articles—it is decreed that an armed attack against one or more of its member nations shall be considered as an attack against all of them and that in such cases all the members are duty-bound to aid the beleaguered country, by force of arms if necessary.

In the aggressiveness of the Stalin regime, people saw an obvious parallel to Hitler's successful coups in the 1930s, when he subjected one country after another to his domination while the rest of Europe was content with the role of the spectator. Here the people of the Western European democracies could see horrifying reminders of the past. And they sought to learn from those tragic experiences: they joined forces for mutual defense against the powerful dictatorship in the East. This was being done, it appeared, at the eleventh hour.

Even the Nordic countries appeared to be in the danger zone. In 1948–49 Norway felt the threat from the Soviet Union as imminent. The country had received alarming communiqués from the Kremlin, and great tension prevailed along its northern border. Quite suddenly the foreign minister of Norway's Social Democratic government, Halvor Lange, flew to Washington in February of 1949 in order to apply for admission to the Atlantic Pact. His urgent journey took place under the pressure of the powerful Russian threat. This happened during my first period of residence in America, and I noticed that it was given wide coverage in the American press. The Americans expressed great concern for Norway, their valiant ally from World War II. And obviously the Norwegian foreign minister was coming to Washington on a mission that was vital to his country. The plans for a Nordic defense alliance had fallen through and both Norway and Denmark sought their security in the Atlantic Pact.[1]

Following the defense alliance of these fifteen nations, the situation in Europe stabilized. The expansion from the East came to a halt. The unsuccessful blockade of Berlin in the summer of 1948 was the Soviet Union's final forward thrust while Stalin was still alive.

And the United States became the pillar of the Atlantic Pact, which by virtue of its membership gained such power that it counterbalanced the military might of the East Bloc. The balance of power that then ensued seemed, for the time being at any rate, to ward off the threat to the democratically governed countries of Western Europe.

And at that time I saw the United States, in short, "as the most powerful defender of human freedom in the world." Such was the incontestable view I had of the Land of Our Kinsmen in 1949, when this was written. In the world situation at that time, there was good reason for that characterization.

There is no reason for it in 1968. Twenty years later such catastrophic events have taken place in world politics that even the United States stands out as an aggressive power.

What I have written earlier about America's involvement in Vietnam will not be repeated here, only referred to. In an article in the newspaper *Arbetaren* (August 19, 1965) and in another in *Dagens Nyheter* ("Våld i Öst och Väst" [Aggression East and West], September 1, 1966), I have clearly expressed the opinion that the Americans should pull out of Vietnam and leave it up to the people of that country to decide their own fate. I do not feel that America has in fact any acceptable reasons for waging war in Asia. I cannot see the intervention in Vietnam in any way as a defensive war on the part of the United States. The vast continent of America is not in any way threatened by the people of North Vietnam, even if their government is communistic. The Americans do not even have a common border with North Vietnam anywhere. In other words, there can be no question of self-defense here. Why then is America sacrificing the lives of its young men in Asia?

By this time we ought to have seen through one of the biggest and most disastrous lies in world history: the assertion that a people can defend its homeland by attacking other peoples, that its homeland can be defended even in other countries. No one in the world today should let himself be fooled by this downright false excuse for starting a war: "Our neighbor is threatening us, so let's attack him! Prevention is better than a cure!"

With this excuse, for this alleged reason, many bloody wars have been started during the ages and immeasurable suffering has been caused. We have several examples from Swedish history. One might mention Karl X Gustav's military campaign in Poland in 1656, and Gustav III's attack on Russia in 1788. Not to speak of all of Karl XII's military operations: for eighteen years, 1700–1718, he did nothing but wage war in the defense of his homeland! He defended Sweden in Denmark, Germany, Poland,

Russia, Turkey, and finally in Norway, where he fell, to the great good fortune of the destitute Swedish people who had faithfully and obediently followed him during his many military campaigns.[2]

Even in the 1930s, Hitler used the threat of invasion from his intended victims as an excuse for attacking. But does humankind not have sufficient experience of this false cause of war? Does it still want to be deceived by it?

No, the American military has no business in Asia. Anyhow, the Americans have enough to do in their own country. They ought to leave Vietnam to the people of that country and devote their time to their own affairs. The Americans have extremely difficult social problems to take care of in their own country, which daily occurrences bear witness to.

The war in Vietnam is continuing on now in its fourth year and is costing the United States twenty billion dollars a year. Those are tremendous sums; they might have been used in a better way, but hardly in a worse one. Americans could have used them as aid to the elderly and sick within their own borders, for the cleaning up of the black slum districts, for new and better housing for their own citizens. But with this money they are instead manufacturing bombs that burn down the dwellings of another people. Funds that they could have used for food for their own poor they are using to destroy the crops of poor people in another country and thereby depriving them of food. Money that could have alleviated need and poor conditions in their own country the Americans are using to lay waste to a country located far away in a strange part of the world. It appears to me that the Johnson administration, with its foreign policy, is writing a new chapter to Voltaire's *Candide*, that classic portrayal of human blindness, folly, and cruelty. And the party responsible for this is not a dictatorship but the government of that great, powerful, democratic country on which the Western world has chiefly rested its hopes.

It is calculated that the Americans have dropped more bombs on North Vietnam than the Allies dropped on Germany during all of World War II. Their bombing began in late winter or spring of 1965 and has now been going on for three-and-a-half years. And the victim of it is a primitive country of peasants that cannot reach its assailant in his own land with similar weapons of terror. The greatest military power in the world, the nation most highly developed industrially and technically, is steadily pouring down bombs on North Vietnam's impoverished farmers who are not able to counter their airborne tormentors with the same effective implements of death and destruction: not a single bomb has been dropped on the United States during the years that the war has gone on.

With these facts at hand, who can fail to denounce the United States' war in Vietnam?

Now as a vindication of the Americans' one-sided air war in Asia, a comparison has been made with their bombing of Germany during World War II, which public opinion in Europe's democracies did not react against; on the contrary, it was regarded as necessary for the victory over Hitler. But this comparison is not suitable as an argument here: the Americans entered World War II only after they had been attacked by Japan at Pearl Harbor and Hitler had declared war on them. Then the United States of America was under attack; then the country was fighting a war of self-defense. With the Vietnam War, the situation is completely different; not a single Vietnamese peasant had dreamed of attacking the world's greatest military power when it began dropping bombs over the rice paddies of that country in the year 1965. Concerning the parallel with Hitler's Germany, it should be remembered, furthermore, that the Germans themselves launched the terror bombings against the civilian population as early as the fall of 1940, when they made their all-out effort to destroy London. They had no grounds for their moral indignation when they themselves later had to endure the same kind of warfare. The comparison with World War II must, in other words, be rejected as a vindication of the bombing of Vietnam.

As pointed out, the United States has been the leading power in the Atlantic Pact ever since that defense alliance came into being in 1949. The United States' position of leadership has become more and more pronounced throughout the years, and during the Johnson administration so many strange things have happened here that I ask myself today: What is the goal of the Atlantic Pact nowadays? Is its purpose still the mutual defense of the democratically governed countries of Europe?

Greece has been a member of the Atlantic Pact since 1952. Due to a coup in April 1967, the government of that country was transformed into military dictatorship almost overnight. My immediate reaction in the face of this event was: the United States will not tolerate this violent overthrow of a democratic government that is one of its allies. The Johnson administration continually proclaims that it opposes aggression (as it claims to be doing in Vietnam) and that it is always prepared to see to it that aggression does not pay. A genuine fascist coup has taken place here, and now the United States is going to react at once against the aggressive generals in Athens and see to it that the overthrown government is reinstated. When America has withdrawn its support of the generals' government, it will not live to be many days old. So I believed.

But after one-and-a-half years the military junta is still governing Greece. America has in fact not withdrawn its support of it; on the contrary, the Johnson administration has given it its assistance: the generals have met with the same goodwill as Greece's democratic government. That is why they remain in power. A new dictatorship of unmistakably fascist or Nazi character has been established in Europe, and it has been stabilized with the aid of the United States!

I took it for granted that Greece would be expelled from the Atlantic Pact immediately after the military coup. But the question of the country's expulsion seems not even to have been discussed by the leaders of the alliance![3]

How have these developments been possible? The goal of the Atlantic Pact when it was founded in 1949 was to deter the aggressive Stalinist dictatorship in the Soviet Union from attacking the democracies of Western Europe. Here an attack against one of those democracies has taken place from within, and the Atlantic Pact has held a protective hand over the aggressors so that a new dictatorship has been able to arise within the alliance itself!

And this is happening under the leadership of the United States, which is thereby cooperating in the suppression of human freedom in one of the countries of Europe—the ancient cradle of democracy.

What has happened to the North American republic, which only twenty years ago appeared as a Land of Freedom to people who were fleeing from the tyrants of Europe?

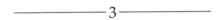

—————— 3 ——————

After this digression I return to the subject of this book, which is indicated by its title: that branch of our nation that resides in North America.

How are our fellow countrymen in the United States of America reacting to the war that their country is waging in Vietnam? What attitude do the Swedish Americans have toward the Johnson administration's aggressive foreign policy, which has increased the risks of a third world war? This writer experiences the fact that these questions need to be asked as a personal tragedy: What position do my own relatives take on this disastrous development? To what degree have they contributed to it, through passivity or in other ways—for does not even passivity involve taking a stand?

The Swedish ethnic group in America, between two and three million people, makes up such a small part of the country's two hundred million inhabitants that its influence on foreign policy or democracy in general is, of course, minimal. And the Swedes' contributions in the political context in the United States, both local and federal, have always been extremely limited: in this respect, they have—in contrast to the Irish, for example—not asserted themselves to an extent that corresponds to their numbers. The Irish are, if anything, overrepresented in politics, while the Swedes have appeared as political leaders only in their own particular areas of settlement, primarily in the Midwest. During certain periods they have had a dominant position in the government of the state of Minnesota. But the country consists of fifty states.

As I indicated in "How the Swedes Become Americans," we find only a small number of our fellow countrymen in the intellectual professions, even if their numbers are on the increase, and we very seldom find them in important political posts. Only on one occasion in the history of the United States has a name of Swedish origin appeared during the election of a president of the great republic. John Albert Johnson, a second-generation Swede and governor of Minnesota, was one of the nominees for the office of president at the Democratic party convention in 1908. He failed to gather enough delegate votes to be nominated and therefore was not involved in the final race itself. He came closer, however, than any other Swede has come—none has made it to the final round.[4]

Minnesota Governor J. A. Johnson was a Democrat, but with his party affiliation he represented only a small minority of his fellow countrymen in the fifty states. The majority of them have, in fact, always felt more at home with the Republicans.[5] In the political attitudes of the Swedish ethnic group, there has not been any change in the one hundred years that have passed since Lincoln's presidency. In the House of Representatives in Washington there are today, 1968, only four members of Swedish origin, three Republicans and one Democrat. This party distribution of three to one would seem to be fairly representative of the Swedish descendants' political sympathies in the United States, but it is probably misleading in that the Republicans' advantage is even greater than what these figures indicate.

I base my assumption on experiences with my American relatives. Of about one hundred relatives in the United States, I have met seventy or more personally, and I have discussed American politics with nearly all of them and especially the selection of a president in their country. During my first long stay in the United States, two presidential elections took place—in 1948 and 1952—which I could follow at close range. As far as I could tell, almost all of my relatives voted Republican: in 1948 they gave their votes to Dewey and in 1952 to Eisenhower. Only three or four of them belonged to the Democratic camp and supported its presidential candidates. Several of my relatives were fierce opponents of Franklin Roosevelt's New Deal; they were convinced that Roosevelt's reform program would lead America into the void.

The Swedish-American voters in the United States belong, in other words, to that class of people in society that by tradition supports the Republican party. This tradition goes all the way back to pioneer days, to the formation of the party in the year 1854, and is associated with the name Abraham Lincoln, its first and—up to now—greatest president. Lincoln was born in a log cabin as the son of a poor settler; he was of the pioneers' own flesh and blood. He was their man and he became their great leader. He formulated the principle of equality with the words: in America one man is just as good as every other and oftentimes he is much better. In 1862 he put through the Homestead Act, which guaranteed every immigrant who wanted to till the soil in America the right to occupy 160 acres of that soil—135 Swedish *tunnland*—without the cost of a cent. Thanks to Old Abe's Homestead Act, the Midwest was settled in a short period of time. We can understand why the unpropertied immigrants—Europe emptied its poorhouses in America—loved Abraham Lincoln, since they were to a great extent farmers without land. The majority of these farmers are still loyal to Abe's party and after a hundred years still give it their votes in presidential elections. They will do so even in 1968. The Midwest comprises one of the Republicans' greatest strongholds, and within this area we have the most bona fide Swedish settlements in the United States.

The fact that the great majority of Americans from the Swedish ethnic group are taking a stand against the Johnson administration in the year 1968 and voting for a Republican presidential candidate does not, of course, entail a demand that the United States should leave Vietnam; instead they feel that the Americans should stay in Asia until they have won the war. Only a year ago Richard Nixon expressed his firm desire to fight and his belief in victory—and for that victory he demanded an even greater use of force: More troops to Vietnam! At that time Nixon was certainly—possibly the situation has changed somewhat since then—a representative spokesman for his party.

The Republican opponents of President Johnson's policies, among whom we must count our kinsmen, are by no means opponents of the involvement in Vietnam itself. But they feel that the war in Asia is badly managed; their dissatisfaction is aimed at the Democrats' way of conducting it: now that America has gotten into the war—for which the Johnson administration bears the responsibility—it must be carried through to a victory.

We want peace in Vietnam—but an honorable and just peace! That is to say: an American peace through victory. That is the platform of the party with which the Swedish descendants feel at home politically.

During my most recent stay in America a couple of years ago, Vietnam was not yet the general topic of conversation among people, but the most alert citizens willingly brought up the subject, which seriously troubled them. Relatives of mine in Chicago—Swedish descendants of the third and fourth generations—proved to be extreme Republicans and expressed amazing opinions. They were young people with college educations and intellectual occupations. Yet they had voted for Barry Goldwater in the last presidential election, and they were very surprised by the astonishment that I showed upon learning this. A young girl, the granddaughter of one of my cousins, who had just graduated from college, formulated her great admiration for Goldwater in glowing terms. To her he was nothing less than the greatest champion of freedom in America! The Republicans had not had a leader of his high caliber since Lincoln. If Goldwater had become president in 1964, then they would not have had this war in Vietnam.

I replied: "Then we would have had the third world war in-stead."[6]

A young man in my circle of relatives, a teacher at North-western University in Evanston, presented an insidious thesis on the causes of all the wars their country had gotten into during the twentieth century. There were four wars, and the instigators of them were four different Democratic presidents: Woodrow Wilson led America into the First World War; Franklin Roosevelt tricked the nation into the Second; and Harry Truman got it into the Korean War. And now Lyndon Johnson, a fourth Democrat, had maneuvered the country into the most unfortunate of all wars, the one in Vietnam. My other relatives concurred enthu-siastically with his conclusion: Every time they got a Democratic president in the United States, they automatically got a war! Couldn't I see from this why they were Republicans and had voted for Goldwater for president?

These young Americans—no Swedish traditions are left, of course, in their generation—were, in other words, not a part of the uneducated populace. They were both gifted and knowl-edgeable, and I had very interesting discussions with them.

Among a great number of people, who can be described as typical of *the man in the street,* I inquired on the same occasion about their views concerning the Vietnam question. They rep-resented a wide range of social groups: they were college grad-uates, white-collar workers, taxi drivers, waiters, housewives, cocktail waitresses, businessmen, and so forth. With only a few exceptions, they believed that the Americans should remain in Vietnam until they had won the war. Their arguments for this attitude can be summarized thus:

During its nearly two-hundred-year history, the United States has not lost a war. (The war of 1812–14 against England ended indecisively, but it was not lost.) The United States has achieved a position as the most powerful democracy in the world today, but with a defeat in Vietnam the nation would lose that position. Even if the Americans withdrew from the battlefields of south-east Asia completely of their own free will, entirely undefeated,

141

the retreat would be regarded as a defeat, brought about by weakness. It would be interpreted as proof that the country was not strong enough to carry the war through to a victorious conclusion. Which would involve such a tremendous loss of prestige for the fifty states of the American union that they could no longer be considered as the leading democratic nation in the world. For this reason above all, the Americans could not leave Vietnam. Somewhere along the line they must stem communist aggression.

And if they withdrew, they would be reneging on their pledge to South Vietnam, to whom they had promised help against the aggression from communist North Vietnam. After this, other friends of theirs, primarily the populations of West Germany and Berlin, would lose their faith in America's promises and its ability to fulfill them.

Against this last argument I maintained that the United States' promise applied to a *democratic South Vietnam*, but the fiction of this ally as a democratically governed country could no longer be maintained. The then President–Prime Minister Ky had already expressed his admiration for Hitler several years before, which should have given the Americans some serious food for thought. America's pledge to give aid had thus been given under conditions that did not exist anymore and could therefore be withdrawn without its possibly being regarded as reneging.

I also pointed out to these American citizens the fact that their involvement in Vietnam had to this point only led to political, military, economic, and—above all—moral setbacks for their country. It was aimed at combating communism but had only served to benefit communism. Aggression from the East had been overshadowed by aggression from the West. Due to America's war in Asia, the Soviet dictatorship had received, for example, much highly undeserved goodwill back home in Sweden. Every assault on human rights in the East Bloc was forgotten or excused in light of the American bombs falling on the people in the peasant villages of North Vietnam. I was of the opinion that the Americans were in actuality carrying on communist pro-

142

paganda in Vietnam. As long as there were American troops in Vietnam, the Johnson administration was unable to react against Soviet intervention in the internal affairs of other countries. It had lost the moral authority that was required to do so.

If that had been in 1968, I would have been able to bring up the Czechoslovakian crisis as a concrete example: so far the United States government has remained silent when confronted with the presence of Russian troops in Czechoslovakia. What can it say?

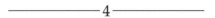

—————— 4 ——————

I acquired my knowledge of the United States mainly during the years 1948–55, when I resided, for the most part, in the Land of My Relatives, working on my novels about the first Swedish emigrants. Since I completed that work—it required twelve years—I have been in America on two occasions for short periods of time in 1960 and 1966.[7] Yet I do not consider the time I have spent in America sufficient to acquire a basic knowledge of that enormous continent, with its many states, so different from one another. There is, undeniably, a great deal that distinguishes Minnesota from Louisiana, Michigan from California, New York from Texas. A person ought preferably to have lived for a while in each of the states in order to acquire a complete knowledge of the country.

Between 1948 and 1950 I wrote many articles for Swedish newspapers in which I recorded my impressions and experiences in America. I am afraid that I made a few altogether too categorical and cockeyed judgments about conditions in the United States. I have probably put forward assertions for which adequate grounds are lacking. After I had lived in the country for a couple of years, I felt as if I knew less about it than upon my arrival. Every experience I had and every adventure I went through was at once confuted by a new experience, a new adventure. So rich, so huge, so multifaceted is this continent that it appears to me impossible to pronounce final judgments about it that lay claim to absolute and general validity. There have been innumerable books about America written by foreigners who have lived only a few months or a year or so in the country, but they are of extremely limited value to a reader who is looking for a realistic and reliable picture of the fifty individual states.

The designation "America, the land of paradoxes and extremes" has been used through the years until it has become trite, and it is still irrefutable. The editor of the first Swedish newspaper in America, the Reverend Hasselquist, found nothing but contradictions in his new homeland, that "highly remarkable country." That was in the year 1854; if Hasselquist were to rise from the grave today, after more than a hundred years, he would probably notice that conditions were unchanged.

Personally I know the Americans as a highly peace-loving people. Any judgment of their general attitude toward violence must read: They despise violence. They hate war and hope for peace, as do all sensible people. They want peace at least as much as any other people, peace for themselves and the world. This is the sum total of my impressions after dealing with them, with private individuals in America. In this nation I have been able to observe, even more than in any other country where I have been, a fear of war, although it has not had any experience of war within its own borders for a hundred years. No one, with good cause, can accuse the Americans in general of worshiping violence.

And yet today they present to the world the image of "a nation of violence," a paradoxical spectacle!

In the year 1854 it struck a sharp-eyed observer like Editor Hasselquist that uprightness, honesty, and love for humanity existed in America alongside "the most fierce bloodthirstiness": "Many times it takes no more than a word before knives start flashing or revolvers go off." A hundred and fourteen years later our fellow countryman's observation still has a familiar ring to those who know the United States only from its appalling gangster films on television, in which the only problem is the question of who will manage to draw his revolver first. But these films certainly reflect one aspect of reality; the most serious kinds of criminality, murder and acts of violence, have spread greatly during recent times.

In this context I ought to mention the statistical data concerning the frequency of crime among different immigrant groups, which were published a few years ago. It was evident from this that the immigrants from the Nordic countries, Swedes, Danes, and Norwegians, could boast of the lowest rate of criminality of all ethnic groups. If the Swedes in America have not made a name for themselves in politics, they have not stood out as criminals either.

In the world of politics, the revolver is still being used as a means of argumentation in the United States: this is a carryover from the Wild West of pioneer days. Four presidents of the North American republic have fallen victim to assassins during the course of the last one hundred years: Lincoln in 1865, Garfield in 1881, McKinley in 1901, and John Kennedy in 1963. And Robert Kennedy, the brother of the last mentioned, was most likely a president-to-be when he was assassinated in June this year. No civilized people would appear to have taken the lives of as many chiefs of state as the Americans.

One symptom of conditions during the 1968 presidential campaign is the strong force of policemen at election rallies and party conventions. Presidential candidates who make appearances have to be protected by lines of policemen three deep, by policemen with precision weapons, tear gas, and helicopters. No one can forget what happened in Dallas, in Memphis, in Los Angeles. One shot can be fired. . . . He who runs today for the position as America's leader is indeed not to be envied: death is waiting for him around every corner.

The highly alarming increase in acts of violence is attributed to an abundant supply of lethal weapons in the country: it is estimated that one hundred million people, every other inhabitant, own a firearm of some sort. This is a state of affairs that must astonish and frighten people and that appears inexplicable to other peoples. But it must be seen—as so much else in the United States—from its historical perspective.

The right to bear arms is the age-old sign of a free man. If we look for its origins in our own backyard, we find them in the history of the Swedish peasant farmer. Swedish farmers always carried arms and thereby showed that they were not serfs. They even took their weapons to church with them, where they were left in a building erected for that purpose next to the church itself. There still remain so-called weapon houses [vapenhus] of this kind from medieval Sweden, where the common men's swords and bows were once kept while the worship service was going on inside the church. The weapons constituted nothing less than a symbol of freedom for the farmer. And he was always prepared to defend his right to carry them. In the year 1520, for instance, Kristian II tried to deprive the Smålanders of their crossbows, but he had to give up the attempt when they responded with an uprising against the king.[8]

When Swedish farmers of a later era emigrated to North America and became pioneers, they naturally preserved their traditional customs regarding the use of arms. Many took their homemade rifles with them to their new homeland, where they were used partly for hunting and partly for defense against assailants and dangerous animals. The Indians do not seem to have been the only danger in the wilderness; bands of lawless white men roamed about murdering and plundering. And it took some years before an effective police force was established in those territories that had just been opened for settlement. In the beginning, therefore, the settlers themselves were compelled to be responsible for law and order, and they administered their own form of justice with their own weapons. The form of administering justice that we know by the designation "lynch law" had its beginnings in primitive pioneer society. It was aimed primarily at Negroes, but both blacks and whites fell victim to it, and many times completely innocent people were put to death by excited mobs.

Thus we have here the origins of the free, unlimited weapons trade in the United States. To the Americans it is a question of an ancient, sacred right, which is protected by the Constitution and that cannot be taken from a citizen of the United States. The many acts of violence in recent times, especially the assassinations of Martin Luther King and Robert Kennedy, have strongly stirred public opinion; more and more citizens want to do away with the open sale of lethal weapons. But every enacted or suggested curtailment of the right to possess arms meets with strong opposition: organizations have been established for the purpose of fighting for this civil right. Therefore I believe that it will be a long time yet before the civilian population of America is disarmed.

In the democratic countries of Europe, like Sweden, for example, the people in general do not have any need for a rifle on their wall or a revolver in their desk drawer. Society has organized and funded a special police force that is charged with the duty of protecting the life, limb, and property of every citizen. But even the United States has a police force that is supposed to maintain law and order and guarantee the safety of the citizens. It appears to us, in other words, that weapons in the hands of civilians would be unnecessary in that country, too. But in this respect old-time pioneer society lives on: a free man has the right to his weapons! And this strange anachronism is kept alive by artificial means through the myth of the Wild West; it is enhanced by a lingering glow from the days of the first pioneers—a romantic view of violence that has cost the lives of many people in that country that I have described as "Europe Transplanted."

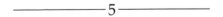

————— 5 —————

The last time I was in America, I saw in Chicago a long protest march, consisting exclusively of young people, who carried a large protest banner with a quotation that was taken word-for-word out of the Declaration of Independence of the United States:

those famous sentences that lay down fundamental human rights, the right to life, liberty, the pursuit of happiness, and so forth. With this nearly two-hundred-year-old text on their banner, these young people were registering their protest against the Vietnam policies of President Lyndon Johnson. And I cannot imagine a more effective protest. It made a very strong impression on the spectators on the street, who greeted the protest march with eloquent silence.

Here I saw a new and young America, and despite all of the disheartening experiences I had had this sight inspired me with new hope for the future of that country.

I believe that the United States must do an about-face and look back again, all the way back to the 4th of July, 1776, and try to find a new way for itself, with a starting point in the declaration of freedom which they drew up on that day.

V. M.

Söderäng, Väddö
August, 1968.

PS

The postscript above was finished on the 13th of August. Eight days later the Soviet Union attacked Czechoslovakia with an army of six hundred thousand men.

The reaction in Sweden, in the government as well as among the people, was one of the most extreme surprise and dismay. Swedish public opinion seemed completely stunned on the morning of the 21st of August. Which was highly revealing: *Both the leaders and the people, that is to say, were completely unaware of the fact that the Soviet regime bases its power solely on violence and the absence of freedom and that it can remain in power solely through violence and the absence of freedom.* Freedom had now worked its way into one of the nations of the East Bloc and threatened the continued existence of the Soviet dictatorship. Naturally the men in the Kremlin were forced to resort to their only argument: Force. How could people believe anything else? The occupation was an act resulting from the instinct for self-preservation. What happened had happened many times before; it was all just a repetition of events that are not so far back in time that people ought not to remember them.

Yet the Swedes—and above all their government—had forgotten:

1. In the 1930s the bloody purges of opponents of the government and the murder of several million peasants as a result of the collectivization of Russian agriculture.

2. The treaty of friendship with Hitler and the Nazi regime on the 23rd of August, 1939, and the infamous agreement on the partitioning of plundered Poland.

3. The attack on Finland on the 30th of November, 1939, when the Soviet Union installed the Kuusinen puppet government that was to take power in a Soviet republic of Finland.

4. The attack on and occupation of the three Baltic states—Estonia, Latvia, and Lithuania—in June of 1940 with the subsequent deportation of a large number of their inhabitants.

5. The occupation of seven additional countries in Eastern Europe at the end of the global war.

6. The quelling by military force of the workers' revolt in East Berlin in June of 1953.

7. Soviet tanks in the streets of Budapest, which in November of 1956 crushed the Hungarians' attempt to regain their freedom.

8. The establishment of the Berlin Wall in 1961, the place of execution for refugees from the East German prison.

9. All the verdicts handed down against authors in the Soviet Union during recent years, a continuing, consistent suppression of the freedom of expression.

The Swedish government and people had forgotten all of this by the time of their awakening on the 21st of August, 1968. And if I know the Swedes correctly, their indignation about events in Czechoslovakia this fall will soon subside, just as it happened with their outrage over events in Hungary in November of 1956. As early as February, 1959, after scarcely more than two years, Khrushchev, the hangman of Hungary, was invited to visit Sweden to be honored, celebrated, and wined and dined here. And just before the "liberation" of Czechoslovakia last summer, Kosygin, Stalin's old co-conspirator and collaborating henchman, arrived as Sweden's guest to be honored, celebrated, wined and dined. And after a suitable period of time has passed, a year or two, Sweden's prime minister—Erlander or Palme—will by invitation be paying a return visit to the men in the Kremlin to be honored, celebrated, wined and dined. After that, Kosygin will pay a new return visit to Sweden where, just like last summer, he will assure us that the Soviet Union is opposed to all aggression and all intervention in the internal affairs of other countries, while members of the Swedish government listen to him, politely and respectfully.

Then the normalization—that is to say, the oppression—of Czechoslovakia will be secured and everything will return to normal in Sweden.

With its attack on Czechoslovakia, the Soviet Union, the mother country of communism, has upheld its position as the greatest defender of oppression in the world. During the last three years it has sometimes appeared as if that position would be threatened by the United States. Now the balance has been restored. But the Swedes had for long enough forgotten the aggression from the East because of the aggression from the West. As I wrote prior to the events in Czechoslovakia: *Due to America's war in Asia, the Soviet dictatorship has received much highly undeserved goodwill back home in Sweden.* But shall we now be spared the extolling of that good, peaceable regime in the East? And with the entry of their troops into Czechoslovakia, the Russians have certainly brought the Republican candidate Richard Nixon to the office of president of the United States—the man who has declared: More troops to Vietnam! We shall win in Vietnam!

With Nixon as president of the United States, the prospects for a third world war will brighten further.

V. M.

150

Notes

Notes

The following explanatory notes are intended to acquaint English-speaking readers with persons and conditions in Sweden and among the Swedes in America. This is information not always accessible to readers without a knowledge of Swedish. References made by Moberg to American cultural phenomena and historical events are generally not explained in these notes.

In referring to secondary sources, I have when possible given the titles of works written in English for the aid of readers who wish to study such matters further. Perhaps the best introduction in English to Moberg's life and works is Philip Holmes' *Vilhelm Moberg* (Boston: Twayne Publishers, 1980). A recent general history of Sweden in English is Franklin D. Scott's *Sweden: The Nation's History* (Minneapolis: Univ. of Minnesota Press, 1977).

Recent books in English on Swedish America include: Harald Runblom and Hans Norman, eds., *From Sweden to America: A History of the Migration* (Minneapolis: Univ. of Minnesota Press, 1976); Lars Ljungmark, *Swedish Exodus* (Carbondale: Southern Illinois Univ. Press, for the Swedish Pioneer Historical Society, 1979); Nils Hasselmo, *Swedish America: An Introduction* (New York: Swedish Information Service, 1976).

At points Moberg refers to provinces in Sweden that it may be useful to pinpoint, in those cases they have not been included in the notes: *Halland,* located on the southwestern coast of Sweden, south of Gothenburg; *Hälsingland,* in east-central Sweden north of Stockholm, on the coast of the Gulf of Bothnia, its major town, Hudiksvall; *Skåne,* an agricultural province in deep southwestern Sweden, bordering on Moberg's Småland, principal city, Malmö; *Västergötland* and *Östergötland,* provinces with combined farming and industrial bases, located to the west and north respectively of Småland; *Värmland,* a heavily forested area in west-central Sweden on the border to Norway; *Västmanland,* an agricultural province located to the west of Stockholm.

Småland is a geographical area united by the common history, speech, and folklore of its people. Unlike nearby Skåne and Östergötland, much of Småland is a heavily forested upland region with severe winters and marginal agriculture. Jönköping is the area's largest city.

Readers unfamiliar with Swedish may notice apparent discrepancies in the spelling of some Swedish words in this text, for instance, *swensk* and *svensk* or *Upsala* and *Uppsala.* Important spelling reforms undertaken in Sweden late in the nineteenth century and again in 1906 standardized Swedish orthography. Thus differences in spelling may exist between older and more recent texts.

Roger McKnight

Introduction

1. Magnus von Platen, *Den unge Vilhelm Moberg. En levnadsteckning* [The young Vilhelm Moberg. A biography] (Stockholm: Bonniers, 1978), p. 310.

2. Ibid., p. 28.

3. Ibid., p. 73.

4. These books are entitled *Utvandrarna* [*The Emigrants*], *Invandrarna* [*Unto a Good Land*], *Nybyggarna* [*The Settlers*], and *Sista brevet till Sverige* [*The Last Letter Home*].

5. The first part of *Soldat med brutet gevär* has been published in English translation under the title *When I Was a Child*, tr. Gustaf Lannestock (New York: Alfred A. Knopf, 1956).

6. In an address to the Swedish Pioneer Historical Society, Moberg stated: "The reason [for writing the Emigrant Novels] is very simple: I wanted to write about my relatives in America. The United States I will call the land of relations." Moberg, "Why I Wrote the Novel About Swedish Emigrants," *Swedish Pioneer Historical Quarterly*, vol. 17, no. 2 (Apr. 1966), p. 63.

7. Moberg, "Romanen om Utvandrarromanen" [The novel about the Emigrant Novels], *Berättelser ur min levnad* [Tales of my life] (Stockholm: Bonniers, 1968), p. 294. This chapter is an especially important source on the writing of the Emigrant Novels. A version of it was published in English in the Swedish magazine *Industria International* (1964), pp. 61–74, 140–46, under the title "Why I Wrote the Emigrants." No translator's name was given. The English-language text may be assumed to be Moberg's own.

8. Moberg's sources for the background to his Emigrant Novels, now in possession of the Emigrant Institute [*Emigrantinstitutet*], Växjö, are itemized and discussed in *Utvandrarromanens källor. Förteckning över Vilhelm Mobergs samling av källmaterial* [Sources for the Emigrant Novels. A listing of Vilhelm Moberg's collection of source materials], ed. Ulf Beijbom (Växjö: Emigrantinstitutet, 1972).

9. Moberg published this bibliography of sources at the conclusion of his novels about emigration. Moberg's listing includes works such as: A. E. Strand, *History of the Swedish-Americans of Minnesota*, 3 vols. (Chicago: Lewis Publishing, 1910); and George M. Stephenson, *The Religious Aspects of Swedish Immigration: A Study of Churches.* (Minneapolis: Univ. of Minnesota Press, 1932). This bibliography did not appear with the English translation of the novels. See Moberg, *Sista brevet till Sverige* [*The Last Letter Home*] (Stockholm: Bonniers, 1972), pp. 315–17.

10. Moberg, "Romanen om Utvandrarromanen," p. 313.

11. Ibid., p. 327.

12. Ibid., p. 314.

13. Gustaf Lannestock, *Vilhelm Moberg i Amerika* [Vilhelm Moberg in America] (Stockholm: Zindermans, 1977), pp. 36, 127. Lannestock's comments on Moberg's personality are surely authentic and reliable, since they are based on close daily contact with the author and the extensive Moberg-Lannestock correspondence, which continued up to the year of Moberg's death. Lannestock died in 1983. This correspondence is preserved by the Emigrant Institute, Växjö, in its manuscripts collection.

14. Moberg, "Romanen om Utvandrarromanen," p. 325. Many of these articles also appeared in *Nordstjernan* in New York, which has been an important source for me in collecting them.

15. Moberg, "Romanen om Utvandrarromanen," p. 301. Lannestock writes of Moberg's dislike for the American portrayal of pioneer life: "Vilhelm Moberg expressed his surprise at the false romanticism that surrounded the pioneers in America. Americans in general [Moberg felt] love the exaggerated heroism which is so assiduously cultivated in film and literature. They depict their heroes as saintly heroes even though they were in reality ordinary people of all types." Lannestock, *Vilhelm Moberg*, p. 40.

16. Lannestock, *Vilhelm Moberg*, p. 13.

17. Originally published in *Dagens Nyheter* in Stockholm, the interview reappeared as: Sven Åhman, "Vilhelm Moberg ser på USA" [Vilhelm Moberg looks at the United States], *Nordstjernan*, Thurs., May 26, 1949, p. 6.

18. Åhman, "Vilhelm Moberg ser på USA," p. 6.

19. Moberg's observation that California Swedes frequently intermarried with other groups contrasts with the results of formal studies on the subject, many of which have been carried out in the Midwest. Ulf Beijbom reports, for instance, that 72 percent of all second-generation Swedish Americans in 1910 had both parents born in Sweden. A study carried out in Pepin County, Wisconsin, showed that only eight of 244 Swedish-American men there married outside their own ethnic group. Of those eight, seven married Norwegians. The higher rate of intermarriage in California would seem attributable to the fact that Swedes there were fewer in number and relatively more urbanized. Ulf Beijbom, "Swedes," *Harvard Encyclopedia of American Ethnic Groups* (Cambridge: Harvard Univ. Press, 1980), p. 979.

20. Sven Delblanc, "Den omöjliga flykten" [The impossible flight], *Bonniers Litterära Magasin*, vol. 42, no. 5 (1973), p. 266.

21. Moberg, "Romanen om Utvandrarromanen," pp. 329–30.

22. Lannestock, *Vilhelm Moberg*, p. 45.

23. Ibid., p. 61.

24. Moberg, in an unpublished letter to Lannestock, August 23, 1954. The letter is in possession of the Emigrant Institute, Växjö.

25. Moberg, in letters to Lannestock on March 22, 1955, and August 11, 1955. Letters in possession of the Emigrant Institute.

26. Einar Haugen, "Vilhelm Mobergs amerikasvenska 'sammelsurium av orimligheter'" [Vilhelm Moberg's *amerikasvenska*, a 'conglomeration of absurdities'], *Svenska Dagbladet*, May 11, 1960.

27. Moberg explained that the entries in *The Unknown Swedes* were copied incorrectly by one of his assistants from Moberg's own barely legible notes. Moberg apparently failed to proofread the assistant's copy. Moberg, "Utvandrarna vittnar om sitt språk" [The emigrants testify about their language], *Svenska Dagbladet*, Dec. 23, 1960.

28. Helmer Lång, "Moberg, the Emigrant Saga, and Reality," *Swedish Pioneer Historical Quarterly*, vol. 23, no. 1 (Jan. 1972), pp. 22–24. Lång also points out that Moberg is wrong when he writes that Swedish historians up to his time had overlooked the significance of emigration (see chapter 1). According to Lång, there are library records that show Moberg had read works on Swedish history by Emil Svensén, whose book *Svenska historien för svenska folket* [Swedish history for the Swedish people], written between 1918 and 1925, contains a twenty-three-page section on the causes of emigration.

29. Lång, "Moberg," p. 13.

Chapter 1. How the Legend of America Was Created in Sweden

The basic ideas for this chapter first appeared in three articles by Moberg: "How the America-Legend Was Born in Sweden," *The American Swedish Monthly*, Dec., 1948, pp. 6–7 and 40; "Vad visste de första svenska utvandrarna om Amerika?" [What did the first Swedish emigrants know about America?], *Nordstjernan*, Mar. 7, 1949, p. 6; and "Den försvunna släkten" [The vanished relations], *Svenska Dagbladet*, Feb. 8, 1948, pp. 11–12.

1. Since Moberg wrote this first chapter, the population of Sweden has risen to over eight million. The official 1975 census showed the population to be 8,209,000. (*Statistical Abstract of the United States 1982–83* [Washington, D.C.: U.S. Dept. of Commerce, Bureau of the Census, 1982], p. 859.) The 1981 population estimate was 8,323,033. (*The Hammond Almanac* [Maplewood, N.J.: Hammond Almanac, Inc., 1983], p. 671.) The 1985 estimate was 8,348,000. (*The World Almanac and Book of Facts: 1987* [New York: World Almanac, 1987], p. 616).

2. Nathan Söderblom (1866–1931) was a professor of religion at Uppsala University, Swedish archbishop, and a member of the Swedish Academy. Following completion of his doctorate in 1901, he wrote extensively on the history of religions. A part-time farm and forestry

laborer as a youth, he maintained a strong interest in social problems. As archbishop he worked to improve relations between the State Church and working-class organizations. Söderblom's interest in the history of the Swedish immigrants increased in 1890 when he attended an international student conference in Northfield, Minnesota. (See Gardar Sahlberg, *Berömda svenskar från tolv sekler* [Famous Swedes from twelve centuries] [Stockholm: Bonniers, 1981], p. 278; *Svenska män och kvinnor* [Swedish men and women], vol. 7, ed. Oscar Wieselgren and Bengt Hildebrand (Stockholm: Bonniers, 1954], pp. 424–27.) Söderblom discussed Swedish emigration at length in his account of a lecture tour of the United States in 1924. He wrote that emigration "has a special place and an importance in the history of our people that we in Sweden little consider and, in general, hardly fathom." (Nathan Söderblom, *Från Upsala till Rock Island: En predikofärd i nya världen* [From Upsala to Rock Island: A preaching tour in the new world] [Stockholm: Svenska Kyrkans Diakonistyrelses Förlag, 1924], pp. 307, 363).

3. For an edition of Grimberg's work, see *Svenska folkets underbara öden* [The wonderful destinies of the Swedish people], 10 vols. (Stockholm: Nordstedt, 1959–63). See also Hildebrand et al., *Sveriges historia intill tjugonde seklet* [Sweden's history to the twentieth century] (Stockholm 1903–10). In the autobiographical work *Berättelser ur min levnad* [Tales of my life], Moberg identifies his schoolbook as C. T. Odhner's *Fäderneslandets Historia* [The history of the homeland]. Moberg attacks this book for presenting Swedish history in an "ultrapatriotic" and "ultraroyalist" manner. According to Moberg, Odhner wrote that the study of history was only concerned with "those groups and individuals who had accomplished something memorable." Moberg argued that such books were aimed at perpetuating the class structure in Sweden by making the lower classes loyal, unquestioning subjects of the crown. (Moberg, *Berättelser ur min levnad*, p. 294.) C. T. Odhner (1836–1904) was a professor of history at the University of Lund. His textbooks in Swedish history, first published between 1869 and 1872, were used in revised editions in Swedish public schools well into the twentieth century. *Svenska män och kvinnor*, vol. 5, ed. Wieselgren and Hildebrand (Stockholm: Bonniers, 1949), pp. 605–06. See Odhner, *Lärobok i fäderneslandets historia samt grunddragen af Norges och Danmarks historia för skolans lägre klasser* [Textbook in the history of the fatherland as well as basics of Norway's and Denmark's history for grade school classes] (Stockholm: P. A. Norstedt, 1883).

4. The *Emigrationsutredning* commission was appointed by the Swedish crown in 1907 to make a statistical-historical study of the causes of emigration. It was hoped that the group's findings would lead to changes

Notes to Pages 8–9

in Swedish legislation concerning emigration. (*Svensk uppslagsbok* [Swedish encyclopedia], vol. 8, ed. Gunnar Carlquist [Malmö: Förlagshuset Norden, 1948], p. 572.) Gustav Sundbärg (1857–1914), a government statistician and later a professor at Uppsala University, authored large sections of the commission's report, including a supplement entitled *Det svenska folklynnet* [The Swedish national character]. *Svenska män och kvinnor*, vol. 7, pp. 322–24. The *Emigrationsutredning* was published in Stockholm in nine volumes and twenty-one parts between 1908 and 1913. For a complete listing of its contents, see *Register till Emigrationsutredningens publikationer* [A register of the *emigrationsutredning*'s publications], ed. Hedvig Lindeström (Stockholm: P. A. Norstedt, 1914).

5. Linköping is a city in Östergötland. The city's population in 1950, when Moberg wrote this section, was 53,232. Its 1986 population was 79,620. See *Svensk uppslagsbok*, vol. 18, ed. Gunnar Carlquist and Josef Carlsson (Malmö: Förlagshuset Norden, 1951), p. 267; *Statistisk årsbok för Sverige 1986* [Statistical yearbook for Sweden, 1986] (Stockholm: Statistiska Centralbyrån, 1986), p. 21.

6. Until the turn of the century, Sweden had a militia system known as the *indelningsverk*. Under this system, each province supplied one regiment to the Swedish army. The enlisted soldiers did monthly duty amounting to thirty days a year and received payment largely in kind. They were professional soldiers who served until age sixty-five. This system was abolished in 1901, when a new military service law was enacted, requiring 240 days of active duty for all men. The new system was opposed by the Social Democratic party and other working-class groups. See Franklin D. Scott, *Sweden: The Nation's History* (Minneapolis: Univ. of Minnesota Press, 1977), pp. 220–22, 398–400.

7. Before the creation of the modern parliamentary system in Sweden, the *riksdag*, or parliament, was controlled by the Four Estates, that is, the nobility, the clergy, the burghers, and the landowning farmers [*bönder*]. Although they constituted only 6 percent of the population, members of the Four Estates controlled government positions and most of the wealth in Sweden. The change to a representative parliamentary system came in 1866. (Scott, *Sweden*, pp. 387–93.) The Social Democrats came to power in Sweden in 1933 and have remained the dominant political party, although they lost the general elections of 1976. Moberg joined the Young Socialist movement at age eleven and remained loyal to it throughout his young manhood. Later in life he was to denounce the Social Democrats, however, for their excessive bureaucracy and support of the Swedish State Church. (See chapter 5 "The Pioneers' Church," for comments by Moberg on the State Church.) For a discussion of Moberg's interest in the socialist movement, see Magnus von

159

Platen, *Den unge Vilhelm Moberg. En levnadsteckning* (Stockholm: Bonniers, 1978), especially the chapter "Uppväxtår och ungdomstid" [The years of growing and time of youth].

8. The Swedish Pioneer Centennial celebration, attended by eighteen thousand people, was held on June 4, 1948, in Chicago Stadium. The principal speakers included Carl Sandburg, President Harry S. Truman, and Prince Bertil of Sweden. The celebration had been planned earlier than 1948 but was delayed by World War II and problems of the postwar years. See Allan Kastrup, *The Swedish Heritage in America: The Swedish Element in America and American-Swedish Relations in Their Historical Perspective* (Minneapolis: Swedish Council of America, 1975), pp. 646–47.

9. The memorial commemorating Fahlström was erected at Kellogg Boulevard and Robert Street in St. Paul on June 26, 1948. Accounts of Fahlström's life include: L. J. Ahlström, *Femtiofem år i vestra Wisconsin: Historiska skildringar* [Fifty-five years in western Wisconsin: Historical accounts] (Minneapolis: Larson Printing Co., 1924), pp. 61–69; Erik Norelius, "Den förste svensken i Minnesota" [The first Swede in Minnesota], *De svenska lutherska församlingarnas och svenskarnas historia* [The history of the Swedish Lutheran congregations and of the Swedes] (Rock Island, Ill.: Augustana Book Concern, 1890), pp. 537–38; Theodore A. Norelius, "The First Swede in Minnesota," *Pioneer Traces in and Near Chisago Lakes Area* (Stillwater, Minn.: Theodore A. Norelius and the Croixside Press, 1971), pp. 16–21.

10. See Carl August Gosselman, *Resa i Norra Amerika* [A journey through North America] (Nyköping, Sweden: 1835); and Carl David Arfwedson, *Scener i Nord-Amerika ur en svensk resandes minnes-bok* [Scenes from North America from a Swedish traveler's book of recollections] (Stockholm: L. J. Hjerta, 1836). *Hemmen i den Nya verlden* appeared in English as *The Homes of the New World: Impressions of America*, 2 vols., tr. Mary Howitt (London: Hall, Virtue & Co., 1853). Bremer visited the Midwest and described Minnesota in *Hemmen* as a new Scandinavia. She wrote: "What a glorious new Scandinavia might not Minnesota become! Here would the Swede find again his clear, romantic lakes, the plains of Scania rich in corn, and the vallies [*sic*] of Norrland; here would the Norwegian find his rapid rivers; and both nations, their hunting-fields and their fisheries. The Danes might here pasture their flocks and herds, and lay out their farms on richer and less misty coasts than those of Denmark." (Howitt translation, vol. 2, p. 314). Bremer's book is perhaps now best known for this statement, which supports a common notion that the Scandinavians settled in Minnesota because the physical features of that state reminded them of home.

In his text Moberg modernizes the spelling and alters the capitalization in the title of Bremer's *Hemmen*. Bremer's book was issued again by Norstedt, in 1866, under the title *Hemmen i nya Verlden*. The discrepancy between the 1853 and the 1866 editions in regard to wording and capitalization may account for Moberg's rendering of the title without *den* and with only *Nya* capitalized.

11. Before 1840 mobility was limited in Sweden by governmental restrictions on travel. A ban on emigration that had been in force since the eighteenth century was not abolished in Sweden until 1840. In that year, King Karl XIV Johan proclaimed that Swedish citizens wishing to travel abroad no longer needed to deposit money in Sweden to guarantee their return. Up to the year 1860 it was necessary to take out a passport even for domestic travel. *The Biography of a People. Past and Future Population Changes in Sweden* (Stockholm: Swedish Royal Ministry of Foreign Affairs, 1974), p. 66.

12. Unonius' two-volume work was published in an English translation in 1950 under the title *A Pioneer in Northwest America 1841–1858*. It was translated by Jonas Oscar Backlund and edited by Nils William Olsson for the University of Minnesota Press and the Swedish Pioneer Historical Society (now the Swedish-American Historical Society). The publication of Unonius' work was one of the first major projects of the Society, founded in 1948. Unonius himself settled again near Uppsala after his return to Sweden. He lived from 1810 to 1902. The quotations in English from Unonius that appear in this text in chapters 1 and 6 are taken from the Backlund translation, vol. 1, pp. 6 and 7, and vol. 2, p. 5.

13. A former soldier in Sweden, Hans Mattson (1832–93) emigrated from Skåne in 1851 and helped establish the Swedish settlement of Vasa in southeastern Minnesota. He became a leading figure in law and politics in Minnesota. Mattson later worked in Sweden as a recruiter of emigrants for the state of Minnesota. He also served from 1881 to 1883 as the United States consul general in India. Although his last name is spelled in America with one *s*, Moberg here gives the Swedish spelling *Mattsson*. His *Minnen* (Lund: Gleerups, 1890) appeared in English as: *Reminiscences: The Story of an Emigrant* (St. Paul: D. D. Merrill, 1891). The English translation in this text, in chapter 1, from Mattson's *Minnen* is based on that in *Reminiscences*, p. 13.

14. The popular press in Sweden traced its beginnings to the first half of the nineteenth century. In 1830, the industrialist Lars Hierta founded the liberal newspaper *Aftonbladet* in Stockholm. The format of this paper, which was directed toward the common people, was inspired

by popular models from Britain and France. An increase in readership among the lower classes was largely a result of the Swedish universal education act of 1842, which made school attendance through the sixth grade possible for all. Although not everyone was able to take advantage of this law, literacy grew more common after midcentury among the younger generations.

15. Here Moberg generalizes rather freely. Apparently the only emigration society of this type existed briefly in Stockholm around 1840, before the beginning of the Swedish emigration, properly speaking. Cf. Märtha Ångström, "Swedish Emigrant Guide Books of the Early 1850's," American Swedish Historical Foundation, *Yearbook, 1947* (Philadelphia, 1947), p. 23.

16. Long out of print, Bolin's book was reissued in a facsimile edition in Swedish in 1970 by Suecica Rediviva of Stockholm under the title *Beskrifning öfwer Nord-Amerikas Förenta Stater.*

17. The *riksdaler* was the basic Swedish unit of money until it was replaced in 1873 by the *krona.* At midcentury one *riksdaler* was the equivalent of twenty-seven cents American currency. The figure of 700 *riksdaler* cited by Moberg would have equaled approximately $190. Florence E. Janson writes that workers in the western, central, and southern United States between 1840 and 1870 received an average yearly wage of 500 *riksdaler* ($135) with food and lodging. She writes: "This wage is extremely low according to the American labor market of the times. It probably appeared high in the eyes of the Europeans." Florence E. Janson, *The Background of Swedish Immigration, 1840–1930* (Chicago: Univ. of Chicago Press, 1931), p. 238.

18. Rural Sweden in the nineteenth century consisted of a social hierarchy at the top of which were the *bönder,* or landowning farmers. Although these farmers were often of modest means, they enjoyed a certain independence because they were property owners. Below the *bönder* were the *torpare,* often called crofters or cottagers in English but perhaps best described as tenant farmers; the *statare,* who were migrant workers contracted for six months at a time by landowning farmers and paid in kind for their labor; and the *backstugusittare,* who were landless farm workers so named because they lived in isolated rented cottages. Moberg described the living and working conditions of these groups in his book *Småländskt folkliv* [Folkways of Småland] (Stockholm: LTS förlag, 1982).

19. Moberg fails to take note of the emigration in 1845 of the Peter Cassel party of twenty-one persons from Kisa parish in Östergötland to Jefferson County, Iowa, which is considered the real beginning of peasant emigration from Sweden to the United States. See Florence E.

Notes to Pages 19–21

Janson, *The Background of Swedish Immigration, 1840–1930*, pp. 128–32, and the special number of the *Swedish Pioneer Historical Quarterly*, vol. 32, no. 2 (Apr. 1981), on the Cassel party.

20. Readers wishing a complete discussion of Erik Jansson's doctrine, known as Millennial Perfectionism, may refer to Paul Elmen, *Wheat Flour Messiah: Eric Jansson of Bishop Hill* (Carbondale: Southern Illinois Univ. Press, for the Swedish Pioneer Historical Society, 1976). Note that Moberg in his text spells *Jansson* with one *s*, for reasons that are not clear.

21. Johan Arndt (1555–1621) and Anders Nohrborg (1725–1767) were prominent Lutheran theologians. Arndt, a German, emphasized the individual's personal relationship with God and argued against the formalism of many of his contemporaries. The first of his writings to appear in Swedish translation came out in 1647. His views are often said to prefigure the pietistic movements of the nineteenth century. Nohrborg was a Swedish Lutheran minister known for his homiletics, which were first collected and published in 1771. *Svensk uppslagsbok* [Swedish encyclopedia], vol. 2, ed. Gunnar Carlquist and Joseph Carlsson (Malmö: Förlagshuset Norden, 1947), p. 375; vol. 21, ed. Carlquist and Carlsson (Malmö: Förlagshuset Norden, 1952), pp. 120–21.

22. The notion that Gustaf Flack was the first Swede in Chicago is traceable to Erik Johnson and C. F. Peterson in their book on the Swedes in Illinois. Johnson and Peterson state that Gustaf Flack was in Chicago in 1843 running a shop near Clark Street. They write that he returned to Sweden in 1846 and died there in the same year. Johnson and Peterson mention that Gustaf Flack wrote numerous positive letters about America. Eric Johnson and C. F. Peterson, *Svenskarne i Illinois: Historiska Anteckningar* [The Swedes in Illinois: Historical notes] (Chicago: W. Williamson, 1880), p. 233.

Nils William Olsson disputes Johnson and Peterson's claim. Olsson writes that Carl Magnus Flack, Gustaf Flack's brother, settled in Chicago in 1843. Olsson finds no evidence, however, that Gustaf Flack came to Chicago at that time. Olsson, *Swedish Passenger Ship Arrivals in New York, 1820–1850* (Chicago: Swedish Pioneer Historical Society, 1967), p. 55.

It is difficult to trace which source Moberg used for his information on Gustaf Flack. Moberg does not include *Svenskarne i Illinois* among the documentary sources for his Emigrant Novels. See Moberg, *Sista brevet till Sverige* [*The Last Letter Home*] (Stockholm: Bonniers, 1972), p. 315–17.

23. Olof Olsson (1807–46) was from Söderala parish in Gävleborg county in Hälsingland. An early adherent of Erik Jansson's teachings, he converted to Methodism soon after his arrival in America. He left

the Jansson sect after helping Erik Jansson arrange for the purchase of land in Illinois. Olsson settled on a farm outside Victoria, Illinois (near Bishop Hill), in 1846. There he, his wife, and their two children all died before the end of the year 1846. Nils William Olsson, *Swedish Passenger Ship Arrivals in New York, 1820–1850* (Chicago: Swedish Pioneer Historical Society, 1967), pp. 68–69.

24. Recent books on Bishop Hill and its founder by American historians include: Theodore J. Anderson, *100 Years: A History of Bishop Hill* (Chicago, 1946); Michael A. Mikkelsen, *The Bishop Hill Colony: A Religious Communistic Settlement in Henry County, Illinois* (Philadelphia: Porcupine Press, 1972, reprint of 1892 and 1925 editions); Olov Isaksson, *Bishop Hill. Svensk koloni på prärien/Bishop Hill, Illinois. A Utopia on the Prairie*, tr. Albert Read (Stockholm: LT Publishing House, 1969). Although Isaksson's book is Swedish, it has a dual Swedish-English language text. See also Paul Elmen's book mentioned in note 20 above. Isaksson's book describes Jansson's death. Jansson was shot in the courthouse in Cambridge, Illinois, by John Root, a former member of the Bishop Hill colony, in a dispute over the marriage contract between Root and Charlotta Lovisa Jansson, a cousin of Erik Jansson. Isaksson, pp. 126–28.

25. Many of these letters were later published by Albin Widén in his *När Svensk-Amerika grundades* [When Swedish America was founded] (N.p.: Vasa Orden av Amerika, [1961]). See also Widén's *Amerikaemigrationen i dokument* [The emigration to America in documentary form] (Stockholm: Prisma, 1966), which contains a number of letters from Bishop Hill. Some of the Bishop Hill letters from both sources are given in translation in H. Arnold Barton, *Letters from the Promised Land: Swedes in America, 1840–1914* (Minneapolis: Univ. of Minnesota Press, 1975).

26. One Swedish shilling was worth nine-tenths of a cent, United States currency, in the middle of the nineteenth century. Frederick Tilberg, *The Development of Commerce between the United States and Sweden, 1870–1925* (Rock Island, Ill.: Augustana Library Publications, 1929), p. 25.

27. During periods of famine, Swedish commoners were forced to eat bark bread and bark soup. Moberg discusses this "tradition" in his work *A History of the Swedish People*. In the chapter "Our Daily Barkbread," he tells of consulting nutritionists who assured him of bark bread's nutritive properties. *A History of the Swedish People*, vol. I, tr. Paul Britten Austin (New York: Pantheon, 1973), pp. 36–48.

28. For the full text and music for this song, see Robert L. Wright, *Swedish Emigrant Ballads* (Lincoln: Univ. of Nebraska Press, 1965), pp. 133–35, 200.

29. Karl Gustav Ossiannilsson (1875–1970) was a teacher, journalist, and poet. Born of middle-class parents, he was early in his career a champion of the Swedish Social Democratic movement. He broke with the party in 1904. The poem from which Moberg quotes is entitled "Sverge" [Sweden] and appeared in Ossiannilsson's collection of poems "Sverge, fosterländska dikter" [Sweden, patriotic poems]. "Sverge" was written while Ossiannilsson was still in his twenties and in sympathy with the Social Democrats. K.-G. Ossiannilsson, *Samlade dikter, 1900–1905* [Collected poems, 1900–1905], vol. 1 (Stockholm: Bonniers, 1907), p. 3.

Chapter 2. The Life History
of a Swedish Farmer

This chapter is based on an article by Moberg entitled "En svensk farmares levernesbeskrivning" [The life history of a Swedish farmer] that appeared in *Nordstjernan*, Sept. 9, 1948, pp. 6–7.

1. The information Moberg supplies here is slightly incorrect. The average length of these ledgers is 198 pages. The longest, volume 1 (June 23, 1854, to Aug. 31, 1875), consists of 508 pages; the shortest, volume 7 (Aug. 1, 1897, to Mar. 29, 1898), is only 24 pages. The total number of pages written by Peterson is just under 2,000. Roger McKnight, *Moberg's Emigrant Novels and the Journals of Andrew Peterson: A Study of Influences and Parallels* (New York: Arno Press, 1979), pp. 5–6.

2. This would appear to have been not entirely so. Dr. Albin Widén, who served as director of the American Swedish Institute during the early 1940s, stated that he had been familiar with the Peterson diaries at that time.

Peterson's journals also had come to the attention of Americans. *Minnesota History* reported in the March 1940 issue ("Accessions," p. 85) that they had been acquired (as a gift from Peterson's children) by the Minnesota Historical Society. The journal gave a brief description of the contents. Working on a WPA project, Emma Ahlquist completed an English translation of the journals in 1945. This translation is in the Minnesota Historical Society. Also in 1945, Grace Lee Nute published an article on the journals in which she discussed Peterson's writing as a valuable document on the history of Swedish settlement in the Upper

Midwest. Moberg acknowledged Nute's article in his note on Peterson written in 1949 for *Svenska män och kvinnor* [Swedish men and women], vol. 7, ed. Oscar Wieselgren and Bengt Hildebrand (Stockholm: Bonniers, 1954), p. 77. Nute, "The Diaries of a Swedish-American Farmer, Andrew Peterson," American Institute of Swedish Arts, Literature, and Science, *Yearbook*, (Minneapolis, 1945), pp. 105–32.

3. Peterson was known in Sweden as *Anders* not *Andreas*. In the biographical sketch on Peterson that Moberg wrote for *Svenska män och kvinnor* in 1949, Moberg correctly gives Peterson's Swedish name as Anders. Peterson first used the name Andrew when he lived in Iowa in the early 1850s. *Svenska män och kvinnor*, vol. 7, p. 77.

4. As population pressures grew in nineteenth-century Sweden, farms were subdivided among fathers and sons to make room for the younger family members as they married. Many farms were subdivided to the point that they provided only the most meager of livings. A one-quarter unit would be one-fourth of a farm that originally supported one family but had been partitioned into small holdings.

5. In recent years information has come to light, in the form of a diary kept by Peterson in 1850, that shows he emigrated in 1850 at the age of thirty-two and entered America by way of Boston. He traveled to the Midwest via the Great Lakes and found work as an orchard man in Iowa. He lived in Burlington until 1855. McKnight, "Andrew Peterson's Emigrant Voyage of 1850," *Swedish Pioneer Historical Quarterly*, vol. 31 (1980), pp. 3–11.

6. The latest study of this settlement at Waconia is Josephine Mihelich, *Andrew Peterson and the Scandia Story* (Minneapolis: Josephine Mihelich and Ford Johnson Graphics, 1984).

7. Since Moberg wrote this chapter, Nils Hasselmo has published his study of the Swedish language in America. Various terms are used for this mixed language. It has been called *rotvälska, swenglish, svensk-amerikanska, amerikasvenska*. While Hasselmo favors the last term, I have here stayed with Moberg's term *svensk-amerikanska*, or Swedish-American. Nils Hasselmo, *Amerika-svenska: En bok om språkutvecklingen i svensk-amerika* [*Amerika-svenska*: A book about language development in Swedish America] (Stockholm: Esselte Studium, 1974).

8. Einar Haugen has shown that Moberg was correct in his interpretation of *fikade taike*. In standard Swedish the term would be *stickade täcke* [quilted a quilt or crocheted a bedspread]. Haugen has also demonstrated that *kvädlen* is *krädlar*, a Swedish-American verb referring to the use of a device for cradling grain in separating out chaff. Einar Haugen, "Andrew Petersons språk" [Andrew Peterson's language], *Svenska Dagbladet*, Dec. 2, 1960.

Chapter 3. A Swedish Cemetery in America

Moberg wrote a shorter first version of this chapter that appeared as "Svensk kyrkogård i Amerika" [Swedish cemetery in America] in *Nordstjernan*, Aug. 26, 1948, pp. 6–7.

1. Kronoberg County is the location of Moberg's home in Sweden. Located in far south-central Sweden, Kronoberg is part of Småland. Its principal city is Växjö. Kronoberg suffered heavy emigration in the latter half of the nineteenth century. The characters in Moberg's Emigrant Novels came from Ljuder parish, Kronoberg County, and settled in Chisago County, Minnesota.

2. The Center City settlement is one of the oldest in Chisago County. It was founded, as Moberg writes, in 1854, three years after the platting of the county's oldest town, Taylors Falls. The separate groups of Swedes who established Center City were attracted to the area by letters from Eric Norberg, a Swede who lived there temporarily in 1850–51. *A Guide to Swedish Minnesota*, ed. Emeroy Johnson (Minneapolis: Minnesota American Swedish Council, 1980), p. 23.

3. Franconia and Taylors Falls were important in the earliest period of settlement because of the logging industry and their proximity to the St. Croix River. As Moberg writes later in the chapter, the virgin stands of timber in this area were quickly logged out and the communities later became important stops for steamboats bringing immigrants up the Mississippi and St. Croix rivers from Illinois and Iowa.

4. It has not been possible to establish the location of this cabin. However, a similar log building once inhabited by Swedish immigrants and dating from the 1850s has been preserved at Hay Lake, near Scandia, southwest of Taylors Falls.

5. Tyngsryd, Ljungby, and Lessebo are small communities in Kronoberg County. Ljungby is Kronoberg's second largest town, after Växjö. Tyngsryd and Lessebo are small manufacturing centers.

6. Kalmar County borders Kronoberg on the east. Its principal city, Kalmar, is located on the Baltic coast.

7. Småland was especially impoverished in the past due to its rugged highland climate and boulder-strewn landscape, reminiscent in this respect of parts of New England.

8. Moberg is referring here, of course, to the Scandinavian practice of burying the dead in a cemetery (or "churchyard") adjacent to the church. He was obviously impressed by the American habit of situating cemeteries in plots separate from the church building.

9. It is difficult to establish exactly which cemetery Moberg visited. He would certainly have seen the Swedish cemeteries at the Taylors Falls Lutheran Church (1851) and Center City's Chisago Lakes Lutheran Church (1854). It seems likely, however, that he is here referring to an equally old graveyard on the south shore of South Center City Lake. This is known as the Glader Cemetery, named after A. P. Glader who settled in the area in 1853. Theodore A. Norelius, who knew Moberg when the latter visited Chisago County in the late 1940s, writes that Moberg visited this cemetery, made notes about the names and dates on the gravestones, and photographed the site. Norelius adds that by the late 1950s one side of this cemetery had been destroyed by road machinery, the fence torn down, and certain grave markers damaged. Theodore A. Norelius, *Pioneer Traces in and near Chisago Lakes Area* (Stillwater, Minn.: Theodore A. Norelius and the Croixside Press, 1971), p. 10, and "Memories of Vilhelm Moberg at Chisago Lakes," *Swedish Pioneer Historical Quarterly*, vol. 30, no. 1 (Jan. 1979), pp. 53–59. Helmer Lång visited the Glader Cemetery in the 1960s and located the grave of a Jonas P. Falk, born 1793, died 1881. Helmer Lång, "Moberg, the Emigrant Saga, and Reality," *Swedish Pioneer Historical Quarterly*, vol. 23, no. 1 (Jan. 1972), p. 23.

10. In the nineteenth century, Swedes who wished to emigrate were required to gain permission to do so from the Lutheran minister in their home parish. Technically no Swede was allowed to leave his parish without this permission, which the minister entered in the church records. Information found in these records includes the person's name, date and place of birth, knowledge of the catechism and the Bible, and intended destination. Since most emigrants were going to America, this last detail is usually given as *Norra Amerika*. Nils William Olsson, *Tracing Your Swedish Ancestry* (Uppsala: Almquist & Wiksell, 1974), p. 8.

11. In the Swedish military of the past, it often happened that there were too many men in a company with patronymics such as Pettersson or Jansson. To avoid confusion, the inductees were arbitrarily given new names by the enlistment officer. These were the so-called *soldatnamn* [or "soldiers' names"], several examples of which Moberg gives: *Lans* [Lance], *Lif* [Life], *Kron* [Crown], *Rolig* [Funny], *Frost* [Frost], *Strand* [Shore or Beach], *Glad* [Happy], *Bäck* [Creek].

12. The antiquated nature of these Swedish sentences is due primarily to the old-fashioned verb forms used. *I skolen* [you shall] is an older plural form that now would be written as *Ni skall* or *Ni skulle*. *Hafwer hulpet* [has helped] would now appear as *har hjälpt*. In addition, *rolig[het]* is more commonly used at present to mean *funny* or *happy* rather than *peace* or *peaceful*.

13. In standard Swedish the term for *wife of* would be *hustru till* [i.e., "wife to"]. *Hustru af* is a borrowing from English.

14. Moberg has apparently confused the names of this woman, since he names her in the same paragraph first as Lena Stina then as Inga-Lena.

15. Moberg has recalled in *Berättelser ur min levnad* [Tales of my life] (p. 293) how he and two of his friends planned to emigrate to America at age sixteen. Moberg's mother dissuaded him at the last minute. Moberg's friends emigrated, however. Moberg writes that he later learned that one of them died in a railway accident in Michigan.

Chapter 4. "A newspaper with Swedish type . . ."

Moberg published a shorter first version of this chapter under the Swedish title "En tidning med swenska bokstäfwer" [A newspaper with Swedish type] in *Nordstjernan*, Aug. 18, 1949, pp. 6–7.

1. *Skandinaven* was founded under mysterious circumstances. Its publisher and editor was known as Anders Öbom, but as Nils William Olsson has shown this was likely an assumed name, since the real Anders Öbom died in Stockholm in 1850. Olsson argues that the actual name of the newspaper's founder was Napoleon Berger, who is presumed to have emigrated from Stockholm, where he had worked for the liberal newspaper *Aftonbladet*. Berger was under pressure from the Swedish authorities for writings critical of the government and may have emigrated under the assumed name as a result. Nils William Olsson, "Was Napoleon Berger the First Swedish Journalist in America?" *Swedish Pioneer Historical Quarterly*, vol. 3 (1952), pp. 19–29; Erik Gamby, "Napoleon Berger alias Gustaf Öbom," *Swedish-American Historical Quarterly*, vol. 34 (1983), pp. 4–31. For a brief history of the Swedish-language press in America, see J. Oscar Backlund, *A Century of the Swedish-American Press* (Chicago: Swedish American Newspaper Co., 1952).

2. There is evidently some confusion here. T. N. Hasselquist and his associates had planned for a year or more to publish a newspaper which they had decided to call *Den Swenska Posten*. The "first number," dated October 1, 1854, which Moberg claimed to have seen and which he describes as a kind of prospectus, very likely carried that name. However, Moberg points out, below, that in January 1855 the newspaper "changed its name" to *Hemlandet, det Gamla och det Nya* [Homeland, the old and the new]. In actuality, the newspaper began continuous pub-

lication on the 3rd of October, 1854, under the new name from the start. The material that Moberg attributes to *Den Swenska Posten* appeared only thereafter in *Hemlandet*. The name *Svenska Posten* was later used by Swedish-American newspapers in Rockford, Illinois (1911–18) and Seattle, Washington (1936–76). See Bernhard Lundstedt, *Svenska tidningar och tidskrifter utgifna inom Nord-Amerikas Förenta Stater* [Swedish newspapers and journals published in the United States of America] (Stockholm: Norstedt, 1886), p. 1; Oscar Fritiof Ander, *T. N. Hasselquist: The Career and Influence of a Swedish-American Clergyman, Journalist and Educator* (Rock Island, Ill.: Augustana Historical Society, 1931), pp. 26–28.

3. Tufve Nilsson Hasselquist (1816–91) was ordained in Lund in 1839. After his emigration from Skåne in 1852, he joined the Illinois Synod and was later the first president of the Augustana Synod (1860–70). He was also a teacher at the Augustana College Seminary. A long-time critic of the Swedish State Church, Hasselquist became a leader of the conservative wing of the Augustana Synod and an influential supporter of the Republican party in the United States. *Svenskt Biografiskt Lexikon* [Swedish biographical dictionary], vol. 18, ed. Erik Grill (Stockholm: P. A. Norstedt, 1971), pp. 331–32.

4. The Crimean War began on March 28, 1854, when France declared war on Russia in a dispute over the custody of the holy places in Palestine. England later entered the war on the side of France. Sweden concluded a treaty with the allies in 1855 by the terms of which it agreed to make no cessions of territory to Russia in exchange for allied support against Russia. *An Encyclopedia of World History*, ed. William Langer (Boston: Houghton Mifflin, 1962), pp. 633, 727–28.

5. Russia and Sweden were enemies of long standing. The Swedes invaded Russian territory during the reign of Karl XII (1697–1718), in 1788–90 they fought Russia in the Baltic under Gustav III (1771–92), and in 1808–9 Russia conquered Finland from Sweden.

6. Several steps toward complete religious freedom were taken in Sweden during the 1850s. Among these were the abolition of the requirement for public affirmation of faith in 1855 and the repeal of the Conventicle Decree in 1858. The construction of railroads began in Sweden in 1854. By 1862 the line between Stockholm and Gothenburg was completed. Franklin D. Scott, *Sweden: The Nation's History* (Minneapolis: Univ. of Minnesota Press, 1977), pp. 355, 444.

7. The Swedish-American press in general took a stand against slavery in the United States. There seem to have been no Swedish newspapers in America that favored extending the institution throughout the entire country. However, a clear dividing line existed between those

Swedish-American papers that favored its total abolition and those that argued for its containment in the South. Hasselquist was widely known as an abolitionist and a supporter of Abraham Lincoln.

8. Reports on the relative prosperity of the settlements in and around Chisago City vary. F. O. Nilsson, the Baptist minister mentioned by Moberg in chapter 2, reported in 1859 that the future of these towns looked dim. In Chisago City alone he found twenty houses deserted because of the bad economic times. McKnight, "The Journal of F. O. Nilsson: An Early Minnesota Circuit Rider," *Perspectives on Swedish Immigration,* ed. Nils Hasselmo (Duluth: Univ. of Minnesota, 1978), pp. 291–311. Numerous letters to the newspaper describing conditions in early Swedish settlements are given in George M. Stephenson, trans. and ed., "*Hemlandet* Letters," Swedish Historical Society of America, *Yearbook, 1922–23* (St. Paul, 1923), pp. 56–152.

Chapter 5. The Pioneers' Church

Moberg based this chapter on three articles published in Sweden during 1949. They are, in order of publication: "Kyrkoliv i Amerikas svenskbygder" [Church life in the Swedish settlements of America], *Svenska Dagbladet,* Feb. 24, 1949; "Emigranterna och kyrkan" [The emigrants and the church], *Svenska Dagbladet,* Apr. 2, 1949; and "Den vänliga kyrkan" [The friendly church], *Folket i Bild,* no. 50, Dec. 11, 1949, pp. 3, 4, 5, 34, 35, 36.

1. According to Franklin Scott, complete religious freedom did not come to Sweden until 1951. Up to that time, Swedes could not leave the State Church unless they joined another Christian church. This restriction was abolished in 1951. Since Moberg wrote the present chapter in the late 1940s, he was still obliged to be a member of the State Church since he had declared no other affiliation. Scott, *Sweden: The Nation's History,* p. 573.

2. By free churches [*frikyrkor*] Moberg means those churches that were outside the State Church, that is, Methodists, Baptists, and so forth.

3. Moberg refers here to the participation of the Swedish primate, Archbishop Erling Eidem, in the Swedish Pioneer Centennial of 1948.

4. For background, see George M. Stephenson's classic work, *The Religious Aspects of Swedish Immigration* (Minneapolis: Univ. of Minnesota

Press, 1932), which deals much more broadly with Swedish-American culture in general than its title indicates.

5. The Swedish Lutheran clergy in the nineteenth century were required annually to visit the homes of parishioners and quiz them on their living conditions, spiritual matters, and their knowledge of the catechism. This was known in Swedish as the *husförhör* [literally "household examination"]. As mentioned above, parishioners were also required to obtain permission from local clergymen before they could move out of their parishes.

6. Very few Swedish immigrants seem ever to have become Presbyterians and they evidently never organized any Presbyterian congregations of their own. Besides the Augustana Lutheran church, many Swedes joined the Methodist, Baptist, Mission Covenant, Evangelical Free, and Mormon churches.

7. Unlike the State Church of Sweden, which was tax-supported, the Swedish-American churches raised money from private sources, called and dismissed their own clergy, decided on their own format for worship services, and often used lay ministers. Moberg's comments throughout this work indicate that he viewed these distinctive features of the American churches as both a blessing and a curse.

8. Although the earliest Swedish settlers in the Midwest were often served by ministers ordained in Sweden, the Swedish Americans soon founded their own colleges and seminaries for religious and secular education. Many Swedish Americans active in religious circles were strongly influenced by Low Church and Free Church movements brought to America by dissenting groups from Sweden.

Chapter 6. What Do Swedes in Sweden and America Know About Each Other?

This chapter is largely based on two articles by Moberg entitled "Vad vet vi om svenskarna i Amerika?" [What do we know about the Swedes in America?], published in *Svenska Dagbladet*, Oct. 30, 1948; and "Vad vet svenskarna i Amerika om Sverige?" [What do the Swedes in America know about Sweden?], first published in *Svenska Dagbladet*, later in *Nordstjernan*, Jan. 6, 1949, pp. 6–7.

1. See note 2 to chapter 2, above, regarding the Peterson diaries and the extent to which they were known before Moberg read them.

2. Both of these newspapers are still being published in the 1980s,

Nordstjernan in New York and *Svenska Amerikanaren Tribunen* in Chicago, although much of the material in the former is now printed in English. *Svenska Tribunen-Nyheter* [Swedish tribune-news] and *Svenska Amerikanaren* [The Swedish American], both published in Chicago, merged as *Svenska Amerikanaren Tribunen* in 1936.

3. These were all Swedish writers of prose fiction who gained popularity around the middle of the nineteenth century. Blanche (1811–68) portrayed life in Stockholm and spoke for the lower middle class. He is also known for his historical dramas. Schwartz (1819–95) wrote several novels with social motifs. Flygare-Carlén (1807–92), probably the most talented of the four, is best remembered for her novels of the Bohuslän (Swedish west coast) area. She was widely read well into the present century. Edel Lindblom was a popular Swedish writer of sentimental fiction, most of whose works were published in the 1880s and 1890s. For a discussion in English of these writers' periods, see Alrik Gustafson, *A History of Swedish Literature* (Minneapolis: Univ. of Minnesota Press, 1971).

4. Verner von Heidenstam (1859–1940) was a neoromantic novelist and poet who celebrated the Swedish past in his historical fiction. *Karolinerna* [*The Charles Men*] recalls the later years of the *stormaktstid,* Sweden's period of ascendancy in the Baltic during the Caroline era of the seventeenth and eighteenth centuries. The defeat at Poltava of Karl XII, the last of the Caroline kings, by Russia's czarist forces marked the end of Sweden's era as a great military power. Heidenstam, *Karolinerna,* 2 vols. (Stockholm: Bonniers, 1897–98); Heidenstam, *The Charles Men,* trans. Charles Wharton Stork (New York: American Scandinavian Foundation, 1920).

5. Helge Nelson, born in 1882, was a graduate of Uppsala University, professor of geography at Lund University from 1916, and a visiting professor at the University of Chicago in 1926. He is best remembered for his two-volume illustrated work *The Swedes and the Swedish Settlements in North America* (New York: Bonniers, 1943). This work provides an indispensable historical overview of Swedish settlements in the United States and Canada.

6. See chapter 1, note 12, for publication details.

7. These authors were all of the realistic school. Bremer (1801–65) was known in her own time as a leading practitioner of the social novel in Europe. Concerning her travels to (and her account of) America, see Moberg's comments in chapter 1. Berger (1872–1924) returned to Sweden in 1899 after nearly a decade in Chicago and New York. He established himself as a leading Swedish novelist after the turn of the century. See Moberg's comments below on Berger's America stories. Hellström

(1882–1953) lived in New York from 1918 to 1923. Angered-Strandberg (1855–1927) was in America between 1888 and 1894 and wrote about Philadelphia as well as the prairie states. Bremer and Angered-Strandberg tended to be favorably disposed to American society, while Berger and Hellström viewed it less favorably. See Lars Wendelius, *Bilden av Amerika i svensk prosafiktion 1890–1914* [The image of America in Swedish prose fiction, 1890–1914] (Uppsala: Litteraturvetenskapliga Institutionen, 1982).

8. Knut Hamsun (1859–1952), the Norwegian novelist, visited the United States twice in the 1880s, spending various periods of time in Chicago, Wisconsin, Minnesota, and the Dakotas. In 1889 he published in Norway *Fra det moderne Amerikas Aandsliv*, an assessment of American culture in which he criticized American crassness and materialism. He described religion in America as a formalized "faith-ism" and wrote: "America's morality is money." The book has appeared in English as *The Cultural Life of Modern America*, tr. Barbara G. Morgridge (Cambridge: Harvard Univ. Press, 1969). Cf. Harald Naess, *Knut Hamsun og Amerika* [Knut Hamsun and America] (Oslo: Gyldendal, 1969).

9. It is not certain what listing Moberg was referring to. He may, however, have read Ernst Skarstedt's *Våra Pennfäktare* [Our scribblers] (San Francisco, 1897) or *Pennfäktare* [Scribblers] (Stockholm: Åhlén & Åkerlund, 1930). Skarstedt's books contain biographical sketches of Swedish-American journalists, poets, and prose writers, and are still valuable works, though never reprinted.

10. Carl August Sandburg (1878–1967) was born in Galesburg, Illinois, of Swedish immigrant parents. His father, August Danielsson, came to America in 1856 at the age of ten. His mother, Clara Mathilda Andersson, left Sweden in 1873 when she was twenty-three. Both were from Östergötland. (Allan Kastrup, *The Swedish Heritage in America: The Swedish Element in America and American-Swedish Relations in Their Historical Perspective* [Minneapolis: Swedish Council of America, 1975], p. 645.) Sandburg's father left Sweden following the death of his parents and came to Galesburg on the advice of an older cousin, Magnus Holmes, who had emigrated to avoid military service in Sweden. Sandburg's mother seems to have emigrated because of disagreements with her stepmother and through the enticements of America letters she had read. Sandburg has recorded his memories of life in a Swedish-American family in his autobiography *Always the Young Strangers* (New York: Harcourt, Brace and Co., 1952).

11. For a recent appraisal, see Dorothy Burton Skårdal, *The Divided Heart: Scandinavian Immigrant Experience through Literary Sources* (Oslo: Universitetsforlaget; Lincoln: Univ. of Nebraska Press, 1974).

Notes to Pages 96–102

12. Since the early 1960s, Swedish emigration and the Swedes in America have been intensively studied by Swedish historians, particularly at Uppsala University. For their findings, see especially Ann-Sofie Kälvemark, ed., *Utvandring: Den svenska emigrationen till Amerika i historiskt perspektiv* [Emigration: Swedish emigration to America in historical perspective] (Stockholm: Wahlström & Widstrand, 1973); Harald Runblom and Hans Norman, eds., *From Sweden to America: A History of the Migration* (Stockholm: Almqvist & Wiksell; Minneapolis: Univ. of Minnesota Press, 1976).

13. Albert Engström (1869–1940) was a nationally known Swedish regional humorist and caricaturist who wrote largely about the folk culture of Norrland, Roslagen, and Småland. His characters are often picturesque rural types. (Gustafson, *History of Swedish Literature*, p. 335.) Allan Kastrup describes Engström as the writer who was said to have taught the Swedes how to laugh in Swedish (*Swedish Heritage in America*, p. 646).

14. Dalarna is the province in central Sweden, often known in English as Dalecarlia, from which much popular culture and folklore derive. Skansen is the open-air folk museum in Stockholm. Both are popular tourist attractions.

15. *The American Swedish Monthly* was published in New York between 1934 and 1965 by the Swedish Chamber of Commerce of the United States of America.

16. By nearest count, the Swedish-American newspapers still in publication in 1988 are: *California Veckoblad* (Downey, Calif.), *Ledstjärnan* (Vancouver, Wash.), *Nordstjernan-Svea* (Brooklyn, N.Y.), *Svenska Amerikanaren Tribunen* (Chicago), and *Vestkusten* (San Francisco). Only *Svenska Amerikanaren Tribunen* is published mostly in Swedish.

17. Leonard Strömberg (1871–1941), a prolific minor author, was born in Sweden but spent the greater part of his life as a Methodist minister in Nebraska. He wrote more than thirty novels in Swedish with Swedish-American motifs. His books are rags-to-riches tales featuring the rise of impoverished Swedish youths. Strömberg emphasized the value of Christian belief, the ideal of hard work, and small-town virtues. He was widely read in both America and Sweden. See Rita Strombeck, *Leonard Strömberg—A Swedish-American Writer* (New York: Arno Press, 1979).

18. The American Swedish News Exchange was a privately financed organization aimed at disseminating objectively accurate news about Sweden. Naboth Hedin (1884–1973) directed the Exchange from 1926 to 1946. Hedin emigrated from Småland at age sixteen. His major work, co-authored with Adolph B. Benson, was *Swedes in America, 1638–1938*

(New Haven: Yale Univ. Press, 1938). This was a biographical study of prominent Swedish Americans. (*Svenska män och kvinnor* [Swedish men and women], vol. 3, ed. Oscar Wieselgren and Bengt Hildebrand [Stockholm: Bonniers, 1946], p. 357.) Allan Kastrup has published several books on Swedish America, in addition to his journalistic work. Kastrup's most important work is *The Swedish Heritage in America: The Swedish Element in America and American-Swedish Relations in Their Historical Perspective* (Minneapolis: Swedish Council of America, 1975). This is a survey of Swedes in America from the Viking Age to the Vietnam Era. In 1964 the American Swedish News Exchange was replaced by the Swedish Information Service.

19. Selma Lagerlöf (1850–1940) was the Swedish novelist who won the Nobel Prize for literature in 1909. A romanticist, she set many of her tales in her native province of Värmland. *Gösta Berlings Saga* [*The Story of Gösta Berling*] is her best-known novel. Her popular Swedish geography book *Nils Holgerssons underbara resa* [*The Wonderful Adventures of Nils*] has long been a favorite of Swedish schoolchildren.

20. These are names in Swedish literature from the late nineteenth and early twentieth centuries. Erik Axel Karlfeldt (1864–1931) was a leading poet of the 1890s from the province of Dalarna. Pär Lagerkvist (1891–1974) was a novelist who won the Nobel Prize for literature in 1951 for the novel *Barabbas*. Agnes von Krusenstjerna (1894–1940) is best known for her revealing autobiographical novels (The Tony books) about life in the upper classes. See Gustafson, *History of Swedish Literature*, pp. 300–488. (For information on Heidenstam, see note 4 above.)

21. Åbo (known in Finnish as Turku) is a city in southwestern Finland. Its population in 1982 was 163,680, and 4.3 percent of this total consists of native speakers of Swedish. Åbo supports Swedish-language schools and a Swedish-language university. *Finland: Facts and Figures*, ed. Jyrki Leskinen (Helsinki: Otava Publishing Co., 1979), p. 21.

Chicago supported a thriving (mainly amateur) Swedish theatrical life during the period between the 1860s and the 1930s. It largely died out after World War II. Henriette Naeseth lists fifty-one different Swedish-language acting companies in Chicago in her book *The Swedish Theatre of Chicago, 1868–1950* (Rock Island: Augustana Historical Society, 1951).

22. *Facts about Sweden* was an informational booklet published in thirteen editions between 1948 and 1969. It dealt with selected topics including Swedish history, social issues, government, and sport. See, for example, *Facts about Sweden* (Stockholm: Forum, 1969). It was superseded by the publication *Profile of Sweden*.

Chapter 7. The Juniper Bush and the Orange Tree

Moberg took the original motifs for this chapter, that is, the juniper and the orange tree, from his article "Ett möte Småland-Californien" [A meeting of Småland and California], *Svenska Dagbladet*, Feb. 2, 1949. The chapter was also influenced by his later article "Svensk bosättning i den sista nybyggarstaten" [Swedish settlement in the last pioneer state], *Nordstjernan*, Apr. 7, 1949, pp. 6–7, although Moberg included only a few details from this article in his final version of the chapter.

1. Before coming to America to pursue research on his tetralogy of emigrant novels, Moberg found information on traveling conditions in the nineteenth century by visiting Gothenburg's Maritime Museum [*Sjöfartsmuséet*]. Moberg briefly discusses his visit to this museum in *Berättelser ur min levnad* [Tales of my life], p. 300. Ulf Beijbom also supplies illustrated details about sailing conditions in the nineteenth century (details of the type found in the Maritime Museum) in *Drömmen om Amerika* [The dream of America] (Stockholm: Forum, 1971), pp. 41–52.

2. The story of Swedes in California during the Gold Rush has been written in recent years by Ulf Beijbom. Beijbom reports that 162 Swedish-born persons resided in California in 1850. Only 8 percent of California's population were women in that same year. (See Beijbom, *Guldfeber. En bok om guldrusherna till Kalifornien och Klondike* [Gold fever: A book about the California and Klondike gold rushes] [Stockholm: Natur och Kultur, 1979], pp. 64, 85.) United States census figures show 1,405 native-born Swedes resident in California in 1860, out of a total population of 379,994. The 1950 census showed 31,067 persons born in Sweden as being residents of California. This is from a total population of 10,586,213. In 1880, there were 518,176 males and 346,518 females in California. (See United States Bureau of the Census, *United States Census of Population: 1950*, vol. 2, *Characteristics of the Population*, Part 5, California [Washington, D.C.: United States Department of Commerce, 1952], p. 63).

3. The number of California residents born in that state seems to have remained at roughly 50 percent between 1930 and 1980. The 1980 census reported, for example, a total population of 23,667,902. Of these, 10,730,193 were born in California, while 9,123,895 were born in a state other than California. (See United States Bureau of the Census, *1980*

Census of Population, vol. 1, *Characteristics of the Population*, Chapter C, "General Social and Economic Characteristics," Part 6, California, Section 1: Tables 56–155 [Washington, D.C.: United States Department of Commerce, 1983], p. 103).

4. With numerous trips to Sweden and other parts of the United States (and Mexico) interspersed, Moberg lived in or visited California over a period of nearly six years between the late 1940s and the mid-1950s while he completed work on the first volumes of his emigrant novels. He lived mainly in rented homes in the Monterey-Carmel and Laguna Beach areas. Gunnar Eidevall discusses Moberg's whereabouts during this period in *Vilhelm Mobergs Emigrantepos* [Vilhelm Moberg's emigrant epic] (Stockholm: Norstedt, 1974), English-language summary, pp. 333–36.

5. After a period of unemployment in his early twenties, Moberg gained his earliest writing experience during the 1920s as a reporter and editor for small-town newspapers in Östergötland and Småland. Moberg later called this period "my difficult years of apprenticeship." Magnus von Platen, *Den unge Vilhelm Moberg. En levnadsteckning* [The young Vilhelm Moberg. A biography] (Stockholm: Bonniers, 1978), pp. 101–211.

6. The Swedish patronymics are generally spelled with a double *s* indicating the possessive form. Thus the son of a man named Petter [Peter] would have the surname Pettersson, or Peter's son. In standard Swedish, the farmer in question would have written his name Aron Pettersson.

7. Von Platen, in *Den unge Vilhelm Moberg*, gives this man's name as Aron Petersson (1829–75). He died of cholic, leaving behind him, besides 525 *kronor*, a Bible and several other books on religious matters. Von Platen gives his wife's name as Johanna Johannesdotter (1833–1912). Johanna is said to have been one of Moberg's principal sources of information about Swedish folklife in the past. Von Platen, pp. 37–44.

8. The thirty-seven *kronor* and fifty-three *öre* that each of the dead man's children received as his or her share of the estate would have been equivalent in the 1870s to between thirty-five and forty United States dollars.

9. Strangely, Moberg mentions in the paragraphs above that his grandmother could read. Von Platen describes her as unable to read or write. Whatever the case, a common practice in early nineteenth-century Sweden was to teach boys to read and write but to teach girls only to read. Much illiteracy existed, however, among both sexes well into the century. At least one of Moberg's emigrated aunts and uncles was still alive in the United States when he visited America in the late 1940s.

Moberg writes of having met a maternal aunt who had emigrated in 1882. (This was presumably the aunt mentioned in the present chapter.) Moberg reported in 1954 that she had become totally Americanized and remembered only one word of Swedish: *kaffekalas* [coffee klatsch]. Von Platen, *Den unge Vilhelm Moberg,* p. 38.

Chapter 8. How the Swedes Become Americans

Although Moberg states that this chapter was a later composition, large parts of it were clearly based on his article "Det omplanterade Europa" [Europe transplanted], which was published in two parts in *Nordstjernan,* Sept. 8 and 15, 1949, p. 6 and p. 6.

1. Linguistic research of the sort Moberg mentions was subsequently carried out by Swedish scholars. Folke Hedblom recorded Swedish-American speech during three trips to the United States in 1962, 1964, and 1966. The results of his work are now in the *Landsmålsarkiv* [Local Dialect Archives] in Uppsala. In English, Hedblom has written: "The Swedish Speech Recording Expedition in the Middle West," *Swedish Pioneer Historical Quarterly,* vol. 14 (1963), pp. 47–61; "Swedish Speech and Popular Tradition in America: A Report from the Uppsala Tape Recording Expedition, 1964," ibid., vol. 16 (1965), pp. 137–54; and "Research of Swedish Speech and Popular Tradition in America, 1966," ibid., vol. 18 (1967), pp. 76–93. In addition to these scholarly articles, Hedblom gives a lively account of these coast-to-coast travels in the book *Svensk-Amerika berättar* [Swedish America speaks] (Stockholm: Gidlunds, 1982). In 1974 Nils Hasselmo published his study of the Swedish language in America, especially the speech of Swedes in Minnesota. (See chapter 2, note 7.)

2. *Prästgården,* literally "the priest farm," is the Swedish term for parsonage. In the other cases Moberg speaks of, people are confusing provinces with towns, districts, and parishes.

3. This was an association founded in Gothenburg in 1908 to disseminate information about Sweden to foreign countries and to keep Swedes abroad in contact with Swedish culture. Its name has since been changed to *Riksföreningen Sverige Kontakt* [The National Association for Contact with Sweden]. It still has its headquarters in Gothenburg.

4. Moberg is here referring to a theory propounded by certain Swedish writers earlier in the century. These writers argued that Swedes lacked confidence in their own culture and therefore slavishly accepted foreign manners and cultural trends. The foremost proponent of this

theory was Gustav Sundbärg of the *Emigrationsutredning* commission who lamented the emigrants' loss of Swedish customs and rapid Americanization. Sundbärg, *Det svenska folklynnet* [The Swedish national character] (Stockholm: Norstedt, 1911). More recently this idea has been disputed. See especially Sture Lindmark, *Swedish America, 1914–1932: Studies in Ethnicity with Emphasis on Illinois and Minnesota* (Uppsala: Läromedelsförlagen, 1971); Robert S. Salisbury, "Swedish-American Historiography and the Question of Americanization," *Swedish Pioneer Historical Quarterly*, vol. 29 (1978), pp. 117–36. These writers argue that Swedes maintained strong bonds of ethnic solidarity in America.

5. Moberg has apparently produced this quotation from memory or from a faulty translation. It is slightly incorrect in this form. In Williams' text the words are as follows: "But what I am is a one-hundred-percent American, born and raised in the greatest country on earth and proud as hell of it, so don't ever call me a Polack." Tennessee Williams, *Eight Plays* (Garden City: Doubleday, 1979), p. 171.

6. Here Moberg seems to have confused the English terms. "Squarehead" was in fact the usual epithet.

7. In the nineteenth and early twentieth centuries, Swedish-American communities and churches sponsored regular Sunday school classes and "weekday schools" in the summers for instruction in the Swedish language to children. This was seen as complementary to the English instruction given in the American public schools. These Swedish schools declined rapidly after World War I when antiforeign sentiment was strong. For a discussion of this decline, see Nils Hasselmo, *Swedish America: An Introduction* (New York: Swedish Information Service, 1976), pp. 38–41.

8. Gustav III (reigned 1771–92) was the Swedish king, known for his "benevolent absolutism," who did much to bring foreign culture to Sweden during the Enlightenment. He alienated the nobility, however, through his efforts to deprive them of influence and consolidate power around the throne. He was assassinated by disenchanted noblemen. His successor was Gustav IV Adolf, who reigned from 1792 to 1809, when he was deposed by revolution, ending the Gustavian autocracy. (Franklin D. Scott, *Sweden: The Nation's History* [Minneapolis: Univ. of Minnesota Press, 1977], pp. 268–93.) Universal suffrage was established in Sweden in 1918. (Ibid., p. 476.)

9. It seems likely that the professor in question would have been George M. Stephenson (1883–1958), the son of Swedish immigrant parents and a leading historian of both general American immigration and of the Swedes in America.

Chapter 9. Twenty Years Later

This chapter is largely based on information contained in various articles Moberg published in Swedish newspapers during the mid- and late-1960s. Though they were occasioned by the American war in Vietnam and the Soviet invasion of Czechoslovakia, the articles were often aimed at all forms of oppression and military aggression. Pertinent to this chapter are, for example: "Arbetslös bödel" [Unemployed executioner], *Arbetaren*, Jan. 7–14, 1965, in the opinion column "Spetsartikeln" [The debate article]; "Jag får demonstrera—men inte du" [I may demonstrate—but not you], *Arbetaren*, June 24–July 7, 1965, "Spetsartikeln"; "Våld i Öst och Väst" [Aggression East and West], *Dagens Nyheter*, Sept. 1, 1966, pp. 4, 5, 6; "Ofrihetens mäktigaste värn" [Oppression's most powerful defender], *Arbetaren*, Nov. 15, 1968.

1. With Sweden playing the leading role, attempts were made in 1948 to form a Nordic defense alliance, but Denmark and Norway decided against the move because of their doubts about the Scandinavian countries' ability to defend themselves. Norway then joined NATO, followed by Denmark, while Sweden remained nonaligned. Franklin D. Scott, *Sweden: The Nation's History* (Minneapolis: Univ. of Minnesota Press, 1977.), p. 513.

2. Karl X (reigned 1654–1660) invaded Poland by way of Denmark and Germany, penetrating as far south as Krakow. After facing stiff opposition, he withdrew his forces in 1657. Gustav III initiated an ill-fated conflict with Russia in the Baltic. Karl XII (mentioned by Moberg in chapter 6 in connection with Heidenstam's *Karolinerna*) was the last of the great Caroline kings of Sweden. He spent most of his reign abroad on costly military campaigns that drained the Swedish treasury and impoverished the commoners. Long an object of romanticized hero worship by Swedish historians and poets, Karl XII and his reign have since been reconsidered by many writers, including Moberg. Karl XII was killed by an unknown assailant while on a campaign in Norway in 1718.

3. Following several years of unstable democracy in Greece, a group of junior military officers staged a coup on April 21, 1967. The "Colo-

nels"—as the military junta came to be known—set up a military dictatorship and eliminated all restraints to its absolute power. In 1969, the European Commission of Human Rights produced documentation of the regime's torture and harsh treatment of its opponents. Complaints against Greece from several European countries were lodged with the Council of Europe, forcing Greece to withdraw from the Council. Due to American support of the junta, Greece's NATO allies failed to condemn the known injustices. The United States maintained its military aid and good government relations with the military dictatorship until its collapse in 1974. Richard Clogg, *A Short History of Modern Greece* (Cambridge: Cambridge Univ. Press, 1979), pp. 186–99.

4. John A. Johnson (1861–1909) was born near St. Peter, Minnesota, of Swedish immigrant parents. He was elected governor of Minnesota three times between 1904 and 1908. He was nominated as the Democratic presidential candidate by the Minnesota delegation at the Democratic national convention in 1908. Johnson's possible candidacy for the presidency in 1912 was under discussion when he died in 1909. *Dictionary of American Biography*, vol. 5, ed. Dumas Malone (New York: Charles Scribner's, 1961), pp. 104–5.

5. The tendency of Swedish Americans to support the Republican party developed, as Moberg points out, during the last half of the nineteenth century. One source reports that only 10 percent of Swedish Americans voted for the Republicans in 1860. By 1890, however, 90 percent of Swedish Americans supported Republican candidates. One reason given for this development was the conservative political leanings of prominent Swedish-American newspapers such as *Hemlandet*. ("Tuve Nilsson Hasselqvist," *Svenskt Biografiskt Lexikon* [Swedish biographical dictionary], vol. 18, ed. Erik Grill [Stockholm: Norstedt, 1969–71], p. 332.) Hasselquist's surname is normally spelled with a *u*.

6. Moberg's comments on Goldwater, though brief, reflect the strong general opinion in Sweden during the 1960s against Goldwater's aggressive statements on the United States' role in world politics, especially in regard to Vietnam.

7. Moberg revisited the United States in 1966 as a guest of the Swedish Pioneer Historical Society in Chicago. A result of this visit was Moberg's "Why I Wrote the Novel About Swedish Emigrants," *Swedish Pioneer Historical Quarterly*, vol. 17 (1966), pp. 63–77.

8. Kristian II was on the throne of Denmark in the early 1500s when Sweden, under the leadership of Gustav Vasa, won its independence from Danish hegemony. He was called Kristian the Tyrant in Sweden.

Roger McKnight is an Associate Professor of Scandinavian Studies at Gustavus Adolphus College, Saint Peter, Minnesota. He received his Ph.D. degree in Scandinavian Languages and Literatures from the University of Minnesota. Previous publications include *Moberg's Emigrant Novels and the Journals of Andrew Peterson: A Study of Influences and Parallels,* as well as articles in *Scandinavian Studies* and *Swedish Pioneer Historical Quarterly.*